George Alexander Stevens

The Adventures of a Speculist

or, A journey through London: Vol. I.

George Alexander Stevens

The Adventures of a Speculist
or, A journey through London: Vol. I.

ISBN/EAN: 9783337011062

Printed in Europe, USA, Canada, Australia, Japan

Cover: Foto ©Andreas Hilbeck / pixelio.de

More available books at **www.hansebooks.com**

THE ADVENTURES OF A SPECULIST;

OR, A

JOURNEY THROUGH LONDON.

COMPILED FROM PAPERS WRITTEN BY

GEORGE ALEXANDER STEVENS,

(AUTHOR OF A LECTURE UPON HEADS)

WITH HIS

LIFE, a PREFACE, CORRECTIONS, and **NOTES,**
BY THE EDITOR.

EXHIBITING A

PICTURE

OF THE

MANNERS, FASHIONS, AMUSEMENTS, &c.

OF THE

METROPOLIS

AT THE

MIDDLE OF THE EIGHTEENTH CENTURY:

AND INCLUDING

SEVERAL FUGITIVE PIECES OF HUMOUR,
By the Same AUTHOR,

NOW FIRST COLLECTED AND PUBLISHED.

IN TWO VOLUMES.

VOL. I.

LONDON,

PRINTED FOR THE EDITOR: AND SOLD BY S. BLADON,
NO. 13, PATERNOSTER-ROW.

MDCCLXXXVIII.

For their prefervation they are now folely indebted to the care and induſtry which have been employed in the compilation of thefe volumes.—Almoſt thirty years have elapfed fince they originally made their appearance; and then under the moſt unfavourable aufpices were they ufhered forth, having been publifhed in an unfuccefsful periodical work;—a work, to which there were many contributors befide our author, and of which, at no period of its fhort exiſtence, there were known to be even five hundred readers, fupported as it was with all

all the wit, and with all the humour—aye, with all the MANLY
SENSE too—that, in the brighteſt
moments of his literary career, ever
animated the prolific brain of the
mirth-inſpiring GEORGE ALEXAN-
DER STEVENS.

BUT as " the race," we are told,
" is not to the ſwift, nor the battle to
" the ſtrong ;" ſo, even in the midſt
of this diſappointment, GEORGE, far
from being mortified, very *philoſo-
phically*, as well as *poetically*, conſol-
ed himſelf with the ſoothing reflection, that though it is not in *au-
thors*, more than in any other ſet of
poor

poor mortals, to "*command* fuccefs," yet he had himfelf done more——*he had deferved it.*

THE work alluded to appeared, indeed, at a period when Fortune, as yet at war with him in other refpects, feemed determined, that through life he fhould experience nothing *but* difappointment.——— GEORGE, however, knew the jilt he had to deal with, nor was he to be told what a particular delight fhe took in harraffing and hampering WITS; and, while inwardly he defpifed her frowns, tutored by his good genius, he continued with unremitted

ted spirit to court her smiles. Nor was he suffered much longer to court them in vain.—With all the powers of a mind uncommonly active and enterprising, he scorned to be diverted from his purpose by the neglect of a publication, not more unmerited, he was conscious, on his part individually, than by the gentlemen who had embarked with him in it, it was unexpected; and accordingly what, from causes not to be ascribed to himself, the Public had refused to *read*, GEORGE now vowed that the Public should *hear*—hear too from his own lips, in a form more captivating—the form of a *theatrical exhibition!*

HENCE the origin of his ever-memorable LECTURE UPON HEADS, which, but for these very circumstances, untoward as they were, would never, it is possible, have existed; and perhaps it will not be found among the least noticeable recommendations of the present selection, that in most of the pieces of which it consists, the scattered rays are conspicuous of that wonderful constellation of ludicro-moral satire, in the midst of which—aided, it must be confessed, by *wigs and*

and *blocks*—he afterwards shone forth in all his glory.

CERTAIN it is, that no man ever knew better than GEORGE ALEXDER STEVENS—if ever man knew so well—how to " shoot folly as it flies." This was his *hobby*—the hobby of which he formed his *Pegasus*, whenever he chose to amble in the humble paths of Prose, or ventured, though it must be confessed he never ventured far up the arduous steeps of Poetry. Be this as it may, it was a hobby which Nature had taught him to manage with a grace peculiar to himself.

Of this truth, every page that fol--
lows will furnish signal proofs;
proofs, which, with confidence it
may be added, will, to ninety-nine
readers in every hundred, be at the
present period as new, as unexpected, and as welcome, as if they
had never been in being before!—
In fact, surprising as it may appear,
these volumes furnish the only collection that has yet been formed of his
miscellaneous productions; which,
beyond every degree of comparison
(*positive, comparative,* or *superlative,*
as he would himself have phrased
i) are his most valuable ones.

WHAT

PREFACE.

WHAT HOGARTH was with his *pencil*, GEORGE seems evidently to have been with his *pen*. Different as they might be in their talents; or rather, it should be said, in their professional pursuits; in their dispositions there appears to have been a striking congeniality. They each loved themselves to laugh, and to make the world laugh; but amidst all their *fun*, whether upon *canvas* or upon *paper*, they could both, when they chose it, be perfectly *sentimental*, and exhibit *vice*, at one time, in colours as odious, as, at another, they would represent *folly* in colours that were *ridiculous*.

BUT

But, in whaever respects they might agree or disagree, in their several departments, they were confessedly both *original geniuses*; and to the pen of GEORGE ALEXANDER STEVENS the Public is now indebted for an assemblage of pieces exhibiting *(and for the first time exhibiting in one view)* the most *laughable*—without exaggeration too, it may be added, the most *faithful*—picture that ever appeared, of the *manners, fashions, amusements, &c. of London at the middle of the Eighteenth Century.* Though *we*—we, at least, of the *modern* generation of Bucks, who have

the

PREFACE.

the honour to live when that Century begins to approach towards its diffolution—have certainly not a little *refined* upon thofe fafhions, manners, and cuftoms; yet now let it be determined, from a comparative view of the Metropolis at the two periods, how far we have, to any effential purpofe, *improved* upon them.

ACCOUNT
OF THE
LIFE
OF
GEO. ALEX. STEVENS.

HIS origin is not accurately known; but we have been informed that he was born in London, about Holborn. He was the fon of a tradefman, and brought up with a view to fome mechanical employment. The obfcurity of his birth has caft a veil over the early part of his life. Whether diffipation, prodigality, want, idlenefs, profligacy, or inclination, led him to employ his talents in public, we are unable to determine; but the firft notice we meet with concerning him, is as a ftrolling player in one of the provincial companies, whofe chief head-quarters were at

Lin-

Lincoln, where he performed some time *. His own account of himself, extracted from a poem, called 'Religion, or the Libertine Repentant,' 8vo. 1751, affords us every reason to suppose that the tenor of his life had not been much influenced by the rules of piety or virtue. Thus he describes himself:

" By chance condemn'd to wander from my birth
An erring exile o'er the face of earth;
Wild through the world of vice, licentious race!
I've started folly, and enjoy'd the chace:
Pleas'd with each passion, I pursu'd their aim,
Cheer'd the gay pack, and grasp'd the guilty game;
Revel'd regardless, leap'd reflection o'er,
Till youth, till health, fame, fortune, are no more.

* Biographia Dramatica, Vol. I.

Too

Too late I feel the thought-corroding pain
Of 'sharp remembrance and severe disdain:
Each painted pleasure its avenger breeds,
Sorrow's sad train to Riot's troop succeeds;
Slow wasting Sickness steals on swift debauch;
Contempt on pride, pale Want on waste approach."

This poem was written during a fit of illness, and probably made no longer impression than until health returned.

Stevens has been often heard to say, that in the war of (we think) 1739 or 1740, he went aboard a man of war, and used frequently to relate the following story:

During an engagement one of his brother sailors was wounded: another sailor took him in his arms in order to carry him to the cockpit; but before he had brought him off the deck, a

chain-

chain-ball carried away his head, unperceived by the sailor who was bearing him. When the surgeon saw the trunk, he cursed the sailor for bringing him a man without an head. "Damn me (says the fellow) but he had his head on when I took him up."

In the year 1752, Stevens was performing in Dublin; and while there, published a burlesque tragedy, called 'Distress upon Distress,' which does not appear to have been acted.

Stevens established in Dublin "The Nassau Court," over which Sparks, as *Lord-Chief-Joker*, presided. This Court was held in a tavern in Nassau-street. Here subjects of humour were discussed, and all ranks of people were indiscriminately admitted into it to debate on them; but the greatest order and regularity

larity were obferved, fines being always inflicted and exacted for every offence, however trivial, againſt the eſtabliſhed rules. A certain Nobleman, now on the Continent, remarkable for folly and extravagance, having appeared in this Court with his hat on, he was tried for the fame. Juſt as fentence was going to be paſſed on him, his Lordſhip's Advocate ſtarted up and ſaid, " That his client could not be puniſhed for wearing a hat, becauſe it was well known he had no head."

SPARKS has often faid, that STEVENS was the beſt Greek fcholar in England, and feemed to think he had had a college education.

IN the year 1753, STEVENS came to London, and obtained an engagement at
Covent-

Covent-Garden Theatre; where he performed without any applause, which indeed his performances on the stage were in no respect entitled to. In 1754, he published a poem, called ' The Birth-Day of Folly,' in imitation of the Dunciad; but proceeded in the design no further than the first book. In January 1755, the Theatre in the Haymarket was opened with an entertainment ridiculing Macklin's British Inquisition, and called '- The Female Inquisition. By a Lady.' It was supposed to be written by our author, who delivered a Proemium and Peroration; but though aided by the assistance of Miss Isabella Wilkinson's performances on the wire, it ended without any advantage to the adventurers, after being four times repeated.

AT

At this period Mr. STEVENS was celebrated at the feveral convivial focieties then in being, of which there was a great number, as, the Choice Spirits, High Borlace, Comus's Court, &c. and wrote many of the fongs he has fince been applauded for. His finances were generally at a low ebb, and his perfon in durance. He experienced the extremes of mirth and jollity, as well as want and dependance; and led a life, if unftained by crimes, yet defpicable for its meannefs and irregularity. In the year 1754 Mr. STEVENS publifhed in 4to. a Poem, entitled, *The Choice Spirits Feaft*, being a parody on Dryden's celebrated Ode. It feems to have been performed in fome manner by the author, and moft probably in Ireland. He ufually wrote pieces of humour for Shuter, to deliver at his benefit;

benefit; and we believe was the author of a Droll, acted at Bartholomew Fair by that comedian in the year 1759, called, *The French flogged; or, The British Sailors in America.* In 1760, he published a Novel, in two volumes, called, *The History of Tom Fool*; and in 1761 began a periodical publication, entitled, *The Beauties of the Magazines,* in which most of the pieces in these Volumes originally appeared. In 1763 he gave the public some entertainment at the expence of his friend Shuter and Nancy Dawson, in *The Dramatic History of Master Edward, Mrs. Ann, Mrs. Llwnddwhydd, and others, the Extraordinaries of these Times.* 12mo. —For Shuter he composed the first sketch of his *Lecture on Heads*, which is said to have owed its origin to his meeting, in one of his strolling excursions, with a country mechanic who de-

scribed

scribed the members of the corporation with great force of humour. Whether the humour of the piece was not congenial with that of Shuter, or whether he was inadequate to the task, it is certain it was at first scarcely noticed. Luckily for the author, he was prompted to enlarge his plan, and having furnished himself with a complete apparatus, he went into the country, and repeated his *Lecture* with so much success at various places, that he was soon enabled to amass and remit home several large sums of money; by which he secured himself in affluence during the rest of his life.

IN April 1764 he commenced his *Lecture* at the Haymarket, greatly to the advantage of his fortune and reputation. He afterwards travelled over every part of England, Scotland, and Ireland;

Ireland; and even made a trip to North America, and at every place met with the moft flattering and generous reception.

AFTER the *Lecture on Heads* had apparently been repeated often enough to lofe fome of its effect, he compofed another entertainment of the like kind, called *The Supplement, being a new Lecture upon Heads, Portraits, and Whole Lengths.* It began in February 1766; but notwithftanding the author's acknowledged reputation, it was coldly received, and ended with fix nights performance. It was tried again the next year, but with little more fuccefs, being repeated only feven nights.

THE money he had acquired by means of his *Lecture* having made the drudgery of literature unneceffary to him,

him, we do not find that he produced any performance until January 1770, when *The Court of Alexander*, a burletta, fet by Dr. Fifhar, was acted at Covent-Garden with, at leaft, as much fuccefs as either the author or compofer deferved. In 1772, owing to a pirated edition of his Songs being publifhed at Whitehaven, he printed a genuine collection of them at Oxford, in 8vo. In 1773 appeared *The Trip to Porifmouth*, a comic fketch, acted at the Haymarket, confifting of a few detached fcenes, begun and finifhed in five days. He performed in this piece for the laft time himfelf, and afterwards repeated his *Lecture upon Heads* both in London and feveral other places; when, at length, finding his faculties become impaired, he fold the property in his work to Mr. Lee Lewes, a comedian of fome eminence, who endeavoured, but without fuccefs, to catch the fpirit of the original author. The *Lecture upon Heads* will probably never again meet with the favour it formerly obtained.

In 1780, a dramatic performance, called *The Cabinet of Fancy, or Evening Exhibition*, was performed at the Haymarket, and the songs, &c. were printed in 8vo.

It was his misfortune that his mind and body did not keep pace with each other in their decay. He sunk by degrees into a state of all others the most distressing to those who have any connections, either of friendship or consanguinity, with a person so unhappily circumstanced. He retained his bodily faculties after his mind had lost its powers, and exhibited a miserable spectacle of idiotism and fatuity. At length, after remaining several years in this condition, he died at Baldock, in Hertfordshire, September 6th, 1784.

CONTENTS

OF THE

FIRST VOLUME.

VISIT to the FLEET, - Page 4
Various Characters described, with a
New Humbug Song, - 23
HISTORY of EXCHANGE ALLEY, 30
JONATHAN's described, - 55
Parallel between a GAMBLER and a STOCK-
JOBBER, - 69 et seq.
Conversation Scene of a secret Meeting of
STOCKJOBBERS, - 77
A LAME DUCK defined, - 92
VISIT to BEDLAM, - 102
Various Characters described, 110 e. seq.
*AUTHENTIC LIFE of a WOMAN of the
TOWN*, ——— 129
The Mischiefs of a Boarding-School Educa-
tion exposed, - 133
The Dangers of encouraging and indulging
Female Vanity, - 137

Pictures

CONTENTS.

Pictures of Modern Friendship and Family Affection, - - 143
The Arts of Seduction expofed, 148
On Kept Miftreffes and their Keepers, 174
Traits of a Procurefs, - 181
Characters of a Club of Humourifts, 189
Diftreffes of a Street-Walker, - 211
HISTORY OF A REFORMING CONSTABLE, - - 218
JENNY DOUGLAS's defcribed, 243
Miferies of a Bawdy-houfe Proftitute, 245
DESCRIPTION OF WHAT COVENT-GARDEN WAS AND WHAT IT IS, 258

ADVENTURES

OF A

SPECULIST;

OR, A

JOURNEY THROUGH LONDON.

THE reclufe life which inclination led me to purfue at College, attended me at my arrival in this Metropolis. After being fettled fome time in this

this city, my acquaintance were perpetually teizing me to come abroad, and shew myself in the World a little.

I BEGAN to confider what the World was, which they spoke so much about. They had told me LONDON was every thing, and that I should fee such places, and such parties, and enjoy such pleasures, as determined me to make a journey through the Town; but I was determined to travel alone, and whatsoever I met with worth while, like other travellers, resolved to publish.

PLEASING myself all that evening with reflecting on my scheme, I determined to set out the next day; but from what place (as the sailors term it) to take my departure, or what part to pitch upon to make my first day's frolic, I was ignorant: a note, however, sent

me

me next morning; fixed my plan of operations.

" FRIEND TOM,

" AS I find I can't soften my stony-
" hearted creditors, have removed my-
" self to the *Fleet*, where I desire you'll
" call of me: you'll meet some jolly
" chums among us: you need not stand
" much upon the hour of your visit,
" for I shall be at home all day.

Yours,

FRANCIS FLIGHT."

A VISIT TO THE *FLEET*.

ABOUT three in the afternoon I set forward to see my friend. The sight of the iron-grated door chilled me——Sin's opening the gates of Hell (as Milton describes it) came at once into my mind. As the turnkey

——in the keyhole turn'd
Th' intricate wards, and ev'ry bolt and bar
Of massy iron, or solid rock with ease
Unfastens; on a sudden open fly
With impetuous recoil, and jarring sound,
Th' infernal doors, and on their hinges grate
Harsh thunder.

My friend met me in the coffee-room, all spirits, shook me by the hand, swore I was the honestest fellow in England,

land, and then feating me in a box clofe to the window, threw up the fafh, that I might have a profpect into the yard, which was indeed very fpacious, and full of people all differently employed. Here I could not help again having Milton in my mind, where he defcribes the rebellious Spirits amufing themfelves after their downfal.

———Each his feveral way
Purfues, as inclination, or fad choice,
Leads him perplex'd, where he may likelieft fix
Truce to his reftlefs thoughts, and entertain
The irkfome hours.

My friend defired me to look about a little; " and after that," continued he, " I'll take you up ftairs to a very " agreeable party of ladies and gen- " tlemen,

"tlemen, who have chambers upon the same floor with me."

HAVING the door locked upon me on my entrance, the ftrange, difmal, dirty appearance of the infide buildings, the odd looks of the inhabitants, the vaft pleafantry of temper my friend was in ; all thefe affemblages formed fuch a confufion of ideas, that I was bewildered in reflection.

FLIGHT, however, foon roufed me, by pointing to a tall, thin figure, who was walking under the window, in his waiftcoat without fleeves, his hair in a bag, no hat on, deep ruffles at his wrifts, and playing with his fnuff-box.

" THAT man, Tom" (thus my friend began) " that man is a character : he " has been an officer in the army.—My " Lord—a——what's his name, got him

"him his commiffion, but he foon
"fold it, and loft the money at play.
"He is a bigot to gaming. It was but
"laft night he loft his laced hat and
"coat in our tap-room, at all-fours,
"and he has never another.—'Tis
"pity—he's a devilifh clever fellow!
"There is not a better man in England
"for carrying on a hum than he is, nor
"one that can cook a beef-fteak better.
"A fcoundrel of a taylor threw him
"in here.

"See he ftops, and fpeaks to that
"little man in the worfted night-cap,
"and dirty banyan. That man was a
"topping jeweller once; but he hap-
"pened to make a fine diamond ring
"for a certain perfon's kept-miftrefs—
"and though you fee what an ugly fel-
"low he is, he always fancied the ladies
"to

" to be fond of him. He took it into his
" head, becaufe fhe was complaifant
" to him, and afked him to ftay break-
" faft, that fhe was in love with him.
" He told this as a fecret to every
" body, that night, in his club:—it
" came to her ears, and to be revenged
" on him, fhe fent a card to him to
" meet her next day. By her beha-
" viour, fhe made him downright in love
" with her, and fhe perfuaded him to
" commence a fine gentleman, buck,
" and brother of the turf; fo that be-
" tween her and Newmarket, he run
" out in 28 months 16000l. befides be-
" ing as much in debt. She went to
" France with her man, who, by the
" by, they fay went fnacks with her
" in the plunder; and he is fent here
" without any hopes (occafioned by
" the

" the folly of his behaviour) ever to
" have his certificate figned.

" Look at that man in the laced
" frock, with holes in his ftockings,
" playing at Nine-holes. He was turned
" out of doors by his father for his
" extravagance and mifbehaviour; when
" a gentleman took pity on him, and
" lent him 500l. on his own note.—
" There was not a man of *more ftricter*
" honour about town than he was: he
" never refufed giving a man fatisfac-
" tion, let the affront be what it would.
" This friend of his had a very fine
" woman to his wife, and Bob here at-
" tended her one night to the mafque-
" rade, and put fome ftuff (he told me
" what it was, but I've forgot it) into a
" glafs of liquor, and it intoxicated her
" for half an hour; fo in that time he
" took

" took her to a Bagnio, and got to bed
" to her.—But she was such an *ignora-*
" *mus,* she told her husband of it; upon
" which he challenged the husband for
" his wife's aspersing his character, and
" they fought, and Bob was obliged
" to beg his life.—The wife, however,
" would never bed her husband again,
" till he had arrested him for the 500
" guineas—and here he's like to be for
" life, I believe; nay he would be
" starved to death here (for somehow
" nobody likes him) only for a secret
" he bought of an hussar to make liquid
" blacking; and the balls he sells just
" keeps life and soul together.

" But see how well yon man with
" the long beard wheels that barrow
" full of filth—You'd think now, that
" he had been brought up to it from
" his

"his childhood, he does it so easy : and
"you would fancy he's old; yet he is
"not quite 27, and once was as smart
"a fellow as ever stood toast-master,
"dressed as jemmy, laid his money as
"well, and kept as good cattle,
"both women and running-horses, as
"e'er a Commoner in all England:
"but he happened to write something
"about the wrong side of Religion,
"only just out of joke once, for he
"believes in the New Testament, to
"my knowledge; for he was sick here
"last week, and he begged I'd read
"to him; and I ne'er saw any body,
"when he believed he was to die, more
"full of devotion than he was ; so
"you know he had no intentions of
"doing harm by his writings. How-
"ever, except just a few of the funny
"sort, all his acquaintance deserted
"him;

"him; every thing went devilish
"wrong; even his servants made no
"scruple to rob him, for they said it
"was no sin to plunder a heathen; and
"his jockies rid booty against him, be-
"cause he was an infidel. The last
"girl that he kept threw him in here
"for 20l. only, which she lent him at
"Epsom; out of a hundred that he had
"given her about fourteen days before,
"to my knowledge. Here the poor fel-
"low has been hellishly off, to be sure;
"every body, but me, huffing him,
"and shaving him about:-nay, he was
"turned out of the Common-side, be-
"cause the people said he did not
"believe in God and Devil; and they
"would not lie near him, for
"fear the Devil should come some
"night to take him away, and by mis-
"take fly off with any of them. To
"keep

" keep him from perifhing, he has been
" made Common-fide fcavenger, and
" the man of the Fives-Court gives
" him fixpence per week, and a new
" broom, to keep the court clean."

Just then a meffage was fent to my friend, that his company was defired above ftairs.

" You muft know," fays he, "that
" I am going to introduce you to fome
" of the higheft geniufes you ever faw.
" One of them is a Colonel, another a
" Knight, another a Gentleman who
" has fpent 20,000l. and there's their
" Women with them. And there's a
" Player there, a droll fellow *, who
" fhall fing you fome funny fongs."

* G. A. Stevens.

As we went up ſtairs, I could not help being ſurprized at the multitude of people we were obliged to crowd through, who were continually aſcending and deſcending, like bees at the door of a hive iſſuing and returning.

I was introduced by my friend to the maſter of the chamber with much ceremony. He was an elderly man, and made ſeveral apologies that he could not ariſe to receive me; for, as he very pleaſantly obſerved, the gout had taken both his feet priſoners. It was but a ſmall room: the uncurtained bed took up one large part of it; the table was cluſtered with bottles, punch-bowl and glaſſes; ſo that it was with much circumſpection, and carefully taking up the ſkirts of my coat, that I, without any damage done, crept cautiouſly to my feat.

FROM

From the room cleanliness had been vanished ever since the floor was laid; the walls had never been spotted by even the splashes of a whitewasher; but here and there were wooden cuts of running-horses, old ballads, dying speeches, and tradesmen's shop-bills, pasted upon the dingy-coloured bricks, like plasters irregularly stuck upon broken heads.

The back of the stove, or grate, had been burnt out, and its vacancy supplied by an old iron dripping-pan: for a fender there was half a broad hoop, which came off the lady of the lodging's washing-tub.

It was, as I afterwards found out, her visiting-day, and she was dressed in all the pride of taste to receive company.

Her

Her face was a little the worfe for fnuff, fretting, and ftrong waters; the uncleanly hand of Sorrow had furrowed her forehead, and the white of her complexion was rather declined from the lilly tint into the curds-and-whey-colour; but her cheeks were bright with rouge, and her eyebrows neatly arched with Indian ink.

Her head was immenfely in tafte, having no other covering than an often-wafhed topknot; her forehead was ornamented with three or four painted paper flowers by way of a pompoon fprig; and her hair was fmoothed back, fleek as the candle greafe could polifh it.

A pair of three-dropp'd glafs earrings kept time to each action of her head; a piece of narrow black ribband

band encircled her neck, on which were tacked fome fpangles, and half a dozen tops of mother-of-pearl waiftcoat buttons, to make up a jewel necklace.

A GARDEN fattin robe-de-chambre, fhortened into a bed-gown, was her upper garment. The lower part of her drefs was a red Porto-Bello petticoat, emboffed with black figures, and flounced round the bottom with a remnant of flowered linen. She wore no handkerchief, becaufe ladies now go moftly open-breafted. Her flippers had a piece of yellow fringe fewed round them, taken from the old valance of a window-curtain. Her fhort apron, as I afterwards heard, was made out of the fore-bodies of an old French filk waiftcoat, which was formerly worn by her friend, in his days of dreffing.

She

She had on a pair of double ruffles, the gauze and edging of which were a little frayed by their being long in wear; however, as she said, they looked tafty, and shewed that the person who wore them had been used to good things.

AMIDST all this apparatus of dress, she preserved that becoming behaviour so conspicuous among persons of distinction, and what indeed is the true sign to know persons of breeding—the look of superiority,—the tossing her head scornfully,—the frown of forbiddance—the leer of approbation, and the majestical disdain—all which she was as perfect in, as if she had never been out of the precincts of the St. James's Academy.

SHE took care to convince us of
her

her dignity now and then, by stopping her lover with, "I wonder, my dear
"—Lord, Colonel, how can you be
" so incongruous"—and all the other familiar interruptions with which married women of much consequence check their husbands conversation before company: not but that the Colonel, as the punch began to sublimate, broke out now and then into a little harsh word or so; as it happened when he asked the Player I just now mentioned for a song, saying, "Do
" sing a song about Humbug. D—n
" me, if I a'n't fond of it."

Lady. " Lord, my dear, how can
" you be fond of such things now-
" a-days! I am sure you have paid dear
" enough already for those fondnesses."

Col.

Col. " Don't be queer, child! " George, I believe you have gone " through more scenes of life than " us all put together."

Lady. " I wonder, Colonel, you can " aſk about ſcenes, as if he was always " to think himſelf in the playhouſe."

Col. " Did you ever hear ſuch a bun- " ter? She has been ſeven years in " the Fleet with me, and don't know " common ſenſe yet—Why I mean " ſcenes of life, Miſs Nicodemus."

Lady. " Well, Colonel, I ſuppoſe " any miſconception that I may be mal- " appropo in—the gentleman is poſ- " ſeſſed of the tranquility of politeſs, " and will excuſe me.

Player.

Player. " Oh, Madam!

Col. " Come—as Macheath says,
" d—n compliments, and drink about.
" Talking spoils company.--Come, let's
" all tell a story, or sing a song—Come,
" let's have a bumper first—Here's
" God bless the King, and give us
" grace."—*(All drink.)*

THE Colonel was dressed in a very strait-haired tye-wig, the knots of which only reached half-way his cheeks, and he seemed in that India fashion where they wore birds' eggs for bobs in their ears.

HIS countenance was deeply tinged with blue and crimson, like streaks upon an Ægyptian pebble, or a piece of lapis lazuli; and his cheeks, nose, and forehead

forehead were enriched with pimples of the true mulberry make and colour.

His coat was defigned out of a green harrateen bed-curtain, lapelled with a piece of yellow fattin. The remnant of his lady's beft petticoat, which fhe had by falling afleep too near the fire burnt and fcorched to that degree that they could only fave a fingle breadth, was employed as a breaft-work for the Colonel.

His beard was about an inch long, and carrotty; but here and there a folitary grey hair briftled out, looking like icicles in dirty thatch. Chalk-ftones ftood pretty thick upon his hands, and his legs were wrapped up in flannels; however, he never baulked his glafs, nor miffed his joke, either upon himfelf,

self, his friend, or his woman. He would out with every thing, and so it would but make a laugh, why what cared he?—for he was always looked upon as a d——d honest fellow, and a fine companion.

AFTER the bumper had gone round, he called for silence; observing, that they were met to be merry, and merry they would be, in spite of all the scoundrel creditors in the universe : " So,
" George, sing a song about Humbug,
" your last new one, and then we
" who can't sing will tell our lives,
" and so we will keep it up as we ought
" to do."

A NEW HUMBUG SONG, *Tune* MASK ALL.

I.

The sages of old, and the learn'd of this day,
About life, and so forth, have said and will say;

, Yet

Yet in spite of their maxims, as things turn about,
Some hum themselves in, and some hum themselves
    out.
                    Sing tantarara a Hum.

II.

With passions and fashions, and this thing and that,
We would be, we should be; but who can tell what;
This world's a large hive, where to labour we're
    come,
But like bees enjoy nothing excepting our Hum.
                    Sing tantarara, &c.

III.

With ladies when Jemmys and Jessamys mix.
They talk and they walk like things of no sex;
Yet even these things sometimes husbands become;
No, no, they're not husbands, for there lies the Hum.
                    Sing tantarara, &c.

IV.

Some men all their youth will live single thro'
    spite;
But when maggots of marriage old batchelors bite,
                    Then

Then they cunningly chuſe their own ſervants—
 but mum,
Inſtead of a maid, they may meet with a Hum.
      Sing tantarara, &c.

VI.

We all in our turns meet with pleaſures and pains;
To be humm'd, and to hum, are our loſſes and
 gains;
When bit we complain, but when biting we're mum,
And—but our bottle is out, boys, and that's the
 worſt Hum.
      Sing tantarara, &c.

AFTER the ſong was ended, and a bumper drank, the Colonel began with, " Come, who's the next? I can't ſing, " ſo I'll ſay.—I don't believe my life will " be worth hearing; however, I have " had fine fun in my time, as Lucy ſays.

" You muſt know, gentlemen, after " I was big enough to be ſent to any of " our

" our Univerfities, my father was
" againft it, my mother wasn't for it,
" and I didn't chufe it——I would
" be jolly. What had a young fellow
" elfe to do, who had fo much *ready* as
" myfelf?

" However, I thought it was proper
" to do fomething with myfelf, fo I
" went into the Army. The fervice then
" wasn't fo fevere as it has been fince.
" At that time a-day three or four re-
" views in the year was all the fa-
" tigue underwent : now, zouns, they
" make nothing of fending noblemen,
" and men of fortune, to the Eaft and
" Weft Indies ; and what's very odd too,
" they like to go. Our Englifh folks
" feem damnably altered, I can tell you ;
" for here we have turned out more brave
" fellows among our men of fortune
" within

" within thefe ten years, than I would
" have laid fix to four there had
" been in the whole nation.

" I WONDER what the devil poffeffes
" people, who have fuch fine eftates,
" or are in the way of keeping it up fo
" jollily at home, to venture themfelves
" in fuch unwholefome places as Africa
" and America, and have themfelves
" fcalped and cut to pieces for their
" country.—Yes, fo would I, to be
" fure!—My country has done great
" things for me, indeed—Clapped me
" up into gaol here, becaufe a parcel
" of mechanics wanted to devour me."

JUST then a Lady of more than ordinary bulk, a new vifitor, was ufhered into the room. By her fize I fhould have fuppofed her to be full fifter to the fat BRIGHT of Malden. She had on a green and gold negligee, treble ruffles, with a large Bruffels lace upon them; her whole drefs was equal to what we might fuppofe was proper for the firft lady of quality upon a Birth-night, and yet fhe only kept a Bagnio in Covent-Garden.

THERE being a deficiency of chairs, fhe fquatted upon the bed. The unufual weight of her figure broke it; when down with a loud crafh backwards fhe tumbled. Shrieking and kicking her heels up, one of her feet met the bottom of a fnuff-box which *Scheme* was that moment holding to his nofe. The duft blinding him, he rofe up ftamping and fwearing: a large boar cat ftarted from underneath the broken bedftead at the fame time, and jumping, frighted, upon the table,

table, overset the punch-bowl, which was just filled with hot water, upon the Colonel's legs. He roared out, his lady started at the noise, and in her hurry to assist her friend, overset the table, bottles, and glasses. With hideous crash all came tumbling together; the Captain swearing, his lady crying, the rest of the visitors scrambling, the parrot squeaking, and a lap-dog yelping.

AMIDST this confusion, my Friend pulling me by the sleeve, whispered me to follow him; and without any apology, or staying to assist the distressed, for he said they would be better by themselves, we went down stairs.

HISTORY of EXCHANGE ALLEY.

THE next day walking through MOORFIELDS, curiosity tempted me to take a view of the inside of BEDLAM. Passing along one of the wards, I heard a voice loudly repeating the following words—" Long, " Long, Scrip, Scrip, Consolidatum, " Consolidandum—Hurra, Bulls and " Bears—D—— Honesty, and send us " bad News by the next Mail, I be- " seech thee."

WHILE I was listening to these incoherences, a very shabby-dressed person came up to me, and calling me by my name, asked me, if I had forgot him ? To be taken notice of in such a manner,

ner, and in such a place, by a man of so very wretched an appearance, I confess alarmed me. He observed it, and not to keep me in suspence, went on in the following manner : " There was a " time, Sir, when you would have been " neither afraid nor ashamed to recol- " lect me.—Sure you have not entirely " forgot me ? Is my face as much al- " tered as my dress ? Not a remnant " of feature left, that you can remem- " ber me by ? My name is SCRIP, Sir. " JONATHAN SCRIP, I used to be called. " —Now I am"——

HE could not proceed, tears stood in his eyes; he turned his head aside, and walked two or three steps from me. For my own part, I was so astonished, that I could only testify my surprize by my silence. On recovering myself, I took
him

him by the hand, and would have made an apology for the badness of my memory; but he interrupted me, saying, " Not at all—not at all---I have been " too long used to distress, now, to " be shocked at an acquaintance not " remembering me."

I DESIRED him to be assured, that it was not with an intent to shun him; and to convince him of it, begged he would accept of a trifle, for the present, just to get himself into a better habit, and meet me in the evening at the Rose, where we used formerly to sup together when I made an occasional excursion to Town from Oxford. I left him immediately, only repeating my request, that he would not fail to be at the Rose at seven.

I HAD

I HAD been accuſtomed to look, a few months before, upon Mr. SCRIP, (who had been my quondam ſchool-fellow) as one of the moſt thriving men in the city of London. He had married a very amiable woman, who brought him 3000l. and he was not at that time addicted to one faſhionable folly, or deſtructive vice; but remarkably temperate, induſtrious, and allowed to underſtand his buſineſs equal to any man in England. I therefore concluded, he muſt have been drawn into very great, or very bad company; that his head had taken a wrong turn; that like many more, who had been undone before him, he had entered with too much ſpirit into horſe-race and hazard parties; and that he had been too fond of betting upon the Turf, until ſome of thoſe geniuſſes diſtinguiſhed by the title

title of KNOWING-ONES, had plundered him. This was the only way I could account for his diſtreſs; for I know no method which could ſo ſuddenly bring on extreme miſery as GAMING.

Mr. SCRIP was punctual to his appointment in the evening, and at my requeſt, gave me the following account of his misfortunes.

" I REMEMBER, Sir, the laſt time
" you dined at my houſe, the ſatisfac-
" tion you expreſſed in ſeeing me, as
" you were pleaſed to ſay, ſo happy.
" I was ſo, indeed. I had a fortune of
" upwards of 8000l. and my buſineſs
" brought me in a neat 900l. per annum
" profit. I ſhall ſay nothing of my
" wife, as you have ſeen her; and you
" uſed, you know, frequently to ſay,
that

" that you could not tell which was
" most agreeable, her person or her
" temper. But was you to see her now,
" Sir, you would perceive a shocking
" alteration indeed!—She is in Bedlam!
" My misfortunes have had such an effect
" upon her, that they have turned her
" brain. Thank Heaven, however,
" she is now better. I have gone eve-
" ry day to enquire after her; but the
" physicians, for these three months,
" would not permit me to see her. I at
" first thought this refusal very cruel,
" but submitted at last to their reasons;
" for they said, as she was returning to
" her senses, if she was to see me in the
" dress I then wore, it perhaps might
" occasion a relapse, and then her cure
" would be impossible.

" This afternoon I have spoke to
" her—I cannot describe our meeting.
—She

" —She begged I would bring you
" to fee her, and I almoft took the li-
" bety to promife her I would."

I ASSURED Mr. Scrip, that he might command any fervice of mine which could contribute to his and his wife's fatisfaction.

HE thanked me, and I faw fatiffaction fpeak in every feature of his face, while he thus went on with his narration.

" A SHORT time after I laft faw you in
" Town, I went into EXCHANGE AL-
" LEY, to fpeak to one of the people
" who ufed JONATHAN's COFFEE-
" HOUSE *. Several of the Brokers knew

* Which has been, fince our author wrote thefe pages in 1762, fuperfeded by the STOCK EX-
CHANGE,

" me, and one among the reſt, an old
" ſchoolfellow of your's and mine, was
" very aſſiduous in explaining to me
" the meaning of the terms made uſe of
" there. After my curioſity had been
" pretty well ſatisfied, I deſired him to
" drink a bottle with me. We went,
" in conſequence, to a tavern, where my
" companion's whole diſcourſe conſiſt-
" ed of the great advantages which
" muſt inevitably accrue to every rich
" man who could and would lay out a
" ſum of money in buying of ſtock.
" He proved it to me (I thought) plain
" as a mathematical demonſtration, that
" every perſon who had caſh to ſpare,
" and could lay it out in the Alley,

CHANGE, an elegant commodious building, at the end of Sweeting's-Alley, erected by the joint ſubſcriptions of ſome monied Stock-brokers.

EDIT.

" might,

"might, nay muſt, in a very few years, amaſs a prodigious fortune." 'For do but conſider, Sir, (thus he ad-dreſſed himſelf to me) how many men I pointed out to you in JONA-THAN's who had not five guineas a-piece capital to begin with—nay, were worſe than nothing, as the ſaying is, who now keep their country-houſes, their equipages, and live like noble-men---nay, I believe, they eat and drink more extravagantly, only by what they get in the Alley. Now, Sir, if theſe perſons can do this, who began without money, what may not that man do who has 5 or 6000l. to go to market with ? Why it was but to-day I got Mr. WELBY 27l. 8s. in leſs than twelve minutes. Pray, what's merchandizing or ſhop-keeping to this ? The dangers of the ſea, the

'villainy

'villainy of factors, falling markets,
'losses at home, are dreadful drawbacks
'upon a merchant's profits; and dead
'stock and bad debts prevent a tradef-
'man's thriving. Are there not many
'dealers who labour through life in all
'the fatigues of busines, and in their
'old age find themselves scarcely 20l.
'before-hand? But in the Alley, Sir,
'with spirit and application, without
'any of the above-mentioned inquie-
'tudes, a man in a year or two is
'certain of making a great fortune,
'provided he has the happiness of
'meeting with an honest broker; for
'that, Mr. Scrip (taking me by the
'hand at the same time) that, Sir, conti-
'nued he, is a misfortune attendant up-
'on the Alley: I am afraid that every
'man who does business in it, is not so
'strictly honest as he ought to be. It is
                                'a pity,

'a pity, it is a shame, indeed, that 'men won't act as men ought. Upon 'my honour I might have been worth 'thousands, where I am now only pos- 'sessed of hundreds, could I have 'brought myself to connive only at 'some combinations; but I despise 'every dirty trick. I don't trump 'up pieces of fictitious bad news. I don't 'sell out for one-fourth, and charge 'it only as one-eighth. No, I am 'above all such schemes; and I wish 'every Broker could say the same with 'as clear a conscience as I do. But, 'Sir, you will excuse me now: I must 'go, I have great business to do this 'evening. I shall be very glad to see 'you at J NATHAN's, and beg you will 'think of what I have told you.'

"I COULD not prevail with the Bro-
"ker

" ker to ſtay any longer, and as he ſaid,
" I did think of what he told me; nay,
" I could think of nothing elſe. Buying
" of ſtock now filled my head, my
" own buſineſs was quite forgot, and I
" was as much altered in my way of
" thinking, as a milk-maid, when the
" Lord of the Manor makes her a pro-
" miſe of marriage.

" THAT night I lay awake, ruminat-
" ing on the ſuppoſed advantages
" which I ſhould receive from Stock-
" jobbing. Next morning I went to
" JONATHAN's, found out my ſchool-
" fellow, ordered him to buy Stock for
" me immediately, being determined,
" I told him, to follow his plan; and
" added, that I might have nothing to
" hinder my ſucceſs, I would carry it
" on with all the ſpirit I was maſter of.

" MY

"My Broker commended me for my resolution, nay congratulated me upon it; telling me, I happened to be at the Alley the best time in the world to come in at; that such a time might not happen again in seven and seven years; and that he was sure I must be a very lucky man, thus to nick it so to a second, as I had done.

"In a short time I had not only drawn all my own capital out of my own business, and put it into the Alley, but also several sums I had borrowed, my credit then being unimpeachable. A month, six weeks elapsed, and instead of those gains I had expected to meet, like the shower of gold in the fine lady's lap, I found I was a considerable loser. I was very uneasy, and told my agent "so;

" so; but he made light of it, and de-
" sired me to have patience. The
" times indeed were at present a little
" bad, but what then? By and by, he
" assured me I should see a turn.

" Then he advised me to shift
" my money from one Stock to ano-
" ther; 'Keep doing, Sir, says he, keep
' but doing, it will all come round in
' the long run.' Now by thus shift-
" ing of my stock, he got a premium
" for every fresh commission; but just
" at that time I took no notice of it."

I could not help interrupting Mr.
Scrip with asking how he, whom I
knew to be a man of sense, so sharp in
managing his own business, and so wa-
ry about every person he was connected
with, could all on the sudden be made
such an egregious Dupe?

He

He told me it was infatuation.——
"Gaming, Sir, is the moſt enticing,
"as well as the moſt pernicious of all
"other vices; and Stock-jobbing, the
"moſt pernicious part of Gaming.
"Avarice, Sir, baſe avarice ſeized my
"ſenſes. I was ſtupified for a time—I
"ſaw in viſion, heaps of gold all my
"own. But now I have recovered my
"ſenſes; that is, ſince misfortune has
"thoroughly awakened me, I find all
"thoſe phantom proſpects vaniſhed, and
"only miſery left me to look on.

"The continual attendance which
"I paid to Jonathan's, prevented
"me from attending to my own bu-
"ſineſs. My clerks grew careleſs,
"my ſervants cheated me, ſtocks kept
"falling daily, and my affairs at home
"grew worſe and worſe.—I now had
"no

" no friend to confult, but my Broker,
" for I had never let my wife know one
" fyllable of my Stock-jobbing tranf-
" actions. I had refolved to furprife
" her at once with a prefent of ten thou-
" fand pounds out of my 'Change-Alley
" profits. I complained to my agent
" concerning my affairs. He advifed
" me to make one bold pufh, in buy-
" ing or felling ftock for time; and
" fo did his friend, a man with whom I
" had often dealt in the Alley, fince my
" embarking in that connection; a very
" fair-fpoken man; one whofe obfer-
" vations upon Honour, Honefty, Prin-
" ciple, Truth, and Friendfhip, were
" the cleareft I thought I ever heard
" in my life; and a man whom I
" believed to be without guile. Stocks
" rifing two and a half the next day,
" they urged me to buy for time a large
" fum;

" fum; and as both affured me that
" the ftocks would keep rifing for
" above a week, which was longer
" than I bought for, I laid it on
" thicker and thicker. But, mercy
" upon me! when the day of payment
" came, I found myfelf ruined.

" I went home with every horror up-
" on my mind, which I think the
" brain is capable of bearing on this
" fide frenzy. I went to bed in an
" agony not to be defcribed; and lay
" fighing for fome time, till my wife,
" who had heard of my Stock-job-
" bing, and feen too often the decay
" of my bufinefs, with all that mild-
" nefs with which amiable women
" can fo tenderly exprefs them-
" felves, begged me not to make my-
" felf uneafy; faid that I fhould hope
" for

" for the best; that, thank God, we
" were young enough surely to repair
" any crosses and losses; that she had de-
" pendencies that I knew to be of con-
" sequence, which she would make over
" to me immediately; and that she
" would part with all she had in the
" world, if it would only contribute
" to make me easy.

" This, Sir, was just pouring oil
" upon fire, or giving a man drams
" when he is light-headed. I felt, if
" possible, ten times more now than
" ever, on reflecting what I had
" brought such a woman to; and I was
" ashamed to own to her what I had
" done.

" At day-break I arose, and rambled
" most part of the day about the fields,
" home

"home being dreadful to me: at
"length, faint with walking, and the
"anxiety of fretting, I went into a
"tavern in Bloomſbury to refreſh my-
"ſelf, and defired the waiter would
"ſhew me into ſome little room,
"where I could ſit without being in-
"terrupted.

"After continuing there about an
"hour, I heard ſome people come in-
"to the next room, and order a bot-
"tle of wine. I inſtantly recollected
"their voices to be thoſe of my Broker
"and *that very honeſt man* his friend.
"I reſolved not to let them know I was
"there, as I had determined to aſk
"them to advance me a ſum of money
"upon my bond, and thought I
"might firſt hear, if they ſhould
"happen to mention me, how I ſtood
"in

" in their opinions, though I did not in
" the leaſt doubt but that they eſteem-
" ed me with the utmoſt ſincerity, as
" they had ſo often declared they did,
" upon their honours.

" As ſoon as the waiter had ſhut
" the door, my Agent obſerved, that
" this was the ſnuggeſt houſe in Town
" for doing buſineſs in, and that many
" good ſchemes had been contrived in it.

' Now you talk of ſchemes, (replied
' the other) pray what do you intend
' to do with 'ſquire SCRIP? I fancy he
' has ſome notion of aſking us to lend
' him ſome money, by what he hinted
' to me laſt week.'

' HAS he? (ſays my Agent) Why
' then he'll find himſelf as much out
' in

' in that notion, as he has been in
' some others.—Do with him! I don't
' know what to do *with* him. I think
' we *have* pretty well done *for* him:
' however, I wish he was fast, for he be-
' gins to be smoaky. I wonder WIL-
' LIAMS the sheriff's officer has not *done*
' him to-day. I advised a friend of
' mine to take out an action against
' him last night for a hundred.'

' PERHAPS he is arrested,' (was the answer.)

' No, no,' (says the first) ' I should
' have heard of it. If he had, he
' would have sent for me; for he be-
' lieves me to be his near and dear
' friend. And so I will be: I'll make
' him a cuckold, if I can.'

' FOR

'For that reason I wish he was laid
up fast; for his wife (returned the
honest man) is one of the finest women
I ever fixed my eyes upon.'

'Why,' (replied my Agent) 'it is
because his wife is so fine a woman,
that I continue to keep him company;
though I know 'tis all up with him,
and I can't get a shilling more by him.
But his wife's cursed queer too; she is
not one of the right sort. However, she must soon come down:
when she has neither home nor habi-
tation, she must do as others do. Money will make the proudest of them
humble.'

'Why, ay,' (replies the companion)
'we have gone snacks in the husband;
now we'll go shares in the wife.'

"I COULD

"I could not liften any longer.—
" How I got into their room I cannot
" recollect; but darting myfelf upon
" them, down went the table, bottle
" and glaffes, and in two minutes I laid
" them both fprawling at my feet;
" for as cowardice is moft commonly
" an attendant upon guilt, thefe were
" two of the rankeft cowards exifting.

" The noife brought in the land-
" lord and fervants, who feized me:
" the two villains were helped up, and
" immediately infifted upon charging
" me with a conftable. One happen-
" ing to be in the houfe, I was carried
" before a Juftice, and as foon as I had
" got rid of the conftable, a bailiff
" took me into cuftody. My credit
" being gone in confequence, of this
" broker, of mine having taken pains to
" whifper

"whisper my affairs about, the next
"day an execution came into my house,
"and my poor wife was in a moment
"left destitute of every necessary. That
"shock, the ill treatment of the offi-
"cers in possession, and my own con-
"finement, had such an effect upon
"her, that she ran distracted; and the
"day I went from the spunging-house
"to prison, she was conveyed to Bed-
"lam.

"It is now but three months past
"since I have been released from my
"confinement, in the condition you
"saw me, Sir; and I have, every day
"since, been at the Hospital to ask
"after my wife; but never, before yes-
"terday, would they allow me to fee
"her."

I PROMISED Mr. SCRIP, whenever the phyfician thought fhe was well enough to bear a vifit from an old acquaintance, that I would pay my refpects to her; and in the mean time told him, that as he had related to me fo much about JONATHAN's, I was determined to go there with him: accordingly the next day we met by appointment, and went into the City together.

As foon as we entered Exchange Alley, it feemed to me, that we were landed upon a new difcovered Continent, whofe inhabitants, by their looks and geftures, and running backwards and forwards, and joftling each other, were as yet uncivilized; efpecially as they jabbered in an unknown language, and their faces fpoke their minds to be all confufion.

BUT

But we were only then attentive to the Overture of the Entertainment; it was not until we were feated in Jonathan's, that we could properly fay we faw or heard any thing worth notice. But then—good gods!—Ye poetical Spirits of Harmony, Politenefs, Literature, and all the other Scientific Genii whofe infpirations fnatch Human Kind from the level of Brutes, and feat them upon Wifdom's throne, none of ye, ye fancy-born immortals, none of you ever yet, I am fure, entered this coffee-room of clamour.

Nothing was to be heard but a continued repetition of " Long, Long, " Long—Navy, Navy, Navy, Navy " —4 per Cents. 4 per Cents.—In- " dia bonds, bonds, bonds, bonds," &c. while a fpruce fpark in the bar, prinked

prinked out like a Sunday apprentice, kept bawling out, " Iſaac Jacobs !— " Mordecai Iſrael," &c. ſo that the babble of Billingſgate, the confuſion among the female retailers of Rag-Fair, the clamours of a Cockpit, and the uproar of Elections, are but ſimple ſounds to the inceſſant outcries in that Coffee-room.

It was with ſome difficulty, and by keeping very cloſe to my friend Scrip, that I could get through the crowd, the room was ſo full; after much ſqueezing, however, we paſſed the Straits, and ſafely landed at the bench under the clock, which by great chance happened at that moment to be empty.

A waiter came up to us primly dreſſed, and pert as a Pimp at the Shakeſpeare,

speare, to know what we wanted; at the same time adding, that we must not stay there without paying 6d. a-piece.

"Very well," my answer was, "there's a shilling for this gentleman "and myself: I suppose we are to have "a dish of coffee?"

"No, Sir, (replies the rascal of a "waiter) no coffee here; and if you "don't like to stay here without cof-"fee, you must go out: you don't "belong here, and there's nobody wants "to have you here."

Although I expected to be shocked at every thing I met with in this place, yet, I confess, this insolence, from such a scoundrel, provoked me to that degree, I was going to knock him down;

down; but Mr. SCRIP stopped my hands, whispering me, "For God's "sake, think where you are; nor be "surprized, when you find yourself "upon a dunghill, you should be "offended with ill scents."

WHILE we were seated in this box, a pock-marked young fellow seated himself without ceremony by me, while another settled himself by the side of SCRIP, making no apology of, "Gentlemen, I hope we don't inter- "rupt you;" or, "Will you give us "leave?" but with an address as indelicate as a couple of Dutchmen, down they squatted, talked about buying and selling for a few minutes, then rose up again, bawling out, "Scrip, "Scrip—Long, Long, Long, Long,"— and

and made two more voices in filling up the cry.

When they were gone, I could not help remarking on the rudenefs of their behaviour. To this my friend replied, that the Stock-jobbers at JONATHAN's were as much ftrangers to modefty and good-manners, as they were to learning and integrity; and that as we only came there to make obfervations, the more odd incidents we met with the better.

Still the noife of their hawking Scrip, and Annuities, and Lottery Tickets, continued, juft as runners cry the Evening Papers; or as black-guards at Newmarket meeting bawl about the lifts of horfes.

A FELLOW

A FELLOW paſſed by us with his under-lip dangling down, which by the thickneſs of it ſhewed that it was too heavy to be brought up to act in contact with the upper one; but as Providence forms nothing in vain, his chin was turned up with a proper curve, for his nether lip's reſting-place.

As I was directing my view to the door, a fellow ſtepped in, ſeemingly in a great hurry; when his foot tripping, he fell forward into the room, and pitched his head againſt a little copper-countenanced pigmy's mouth, who was that inſtant ſqueaking, " Confolds! " Confolds!" Both fell down, and daſhed out of a third perſon's hand a pocket-book; the owner of which, ſtooping to pick it up, received the heel of a very heavy fellow's ſhoe upon four of his fingers:

gers : his fhrieking, and the diminutive who had been thrown down, fwearing at the fame time, added, if poffible, to the diabolical diffonancy.

I was furprized to fee in the room fo many lads, fchool-boys I took them to be, as the eldeft did not feem to have reached his 15th year; and afked Scrip what bufinefs thofe children had there.

" Those, Sir, (he replied) are the
" young fry, who are nibbling about
" the edges of the pool :—by and by
" they will become great pike, like
" their relations, that you fee are con-
" tinually moving up and down. They
" bring thefe novices here fo young,
" to render their tender minds callous
" betimes againft all humane, generous,
" focial

" social sentiments; and by initiating
" them so young into the secret myste-
" ries of Stock-jobbing, these pupils are
" taught to consider the actions commit-
" ted here by their fathers, brothers,
" uncles, or other relations, not as
" villainous, pitiful, or false, but as
" stratagems of trade, which, when
" they come to be men, they must
" put in practice; as by those means
" they will be enabled to keep country-
" houses and post-chariots, relish turtle,
" pine-apples and Tokay, like the senior
" jobbers before them."

The next person we took notice of had his upper lip drawn up by an involuntary grin, which exposed a set of very broad irregular white teeth; and his mouth being of a livid colour, appeared like an old wound, the edges of which were shrunk back, and the bone left bare.

ANOTHER stood with his back to us, with a large bushy bob, frizzed out as stiff as so many entangled wires. When he turned himself to look on us, his face, I am certain, was not above the dimensions of a twelvemonth-old infant, he looked so silly in features, and yet so consequential in caxon. He was talking to a tall Roman-nosed figure, whose cheek-bones stood out like a bruiser's; while his nostrils were charged with such a quantity of snuff, that his upper lip seemed armed with mahogany-coloured whiskers.

CLOSE to him stood a full-fed figure, round-faced, double-chin'd, with small eyes, and a simper upon his face as unmeaning

unmeaning and ideot-like as the he! he! hé! of a milkmaid, when praifed by her betters. He feemed to be very attentive to a pitiful-looking fellow, whofe face was ftrongly wrinkled, bronzed with dirt, and pitted deeply with the fmall-pox, like the profile of a face upon a ruft-impaired medal.

In the next box to us fat a man with as fhabby a bag-wig, as ever poor fhirtlefs ftrolling-player capered Lord Foppington in. His companion wore his own hair, if the hair was worth owning; for it was as fhort as his ears, and the thinneft crop I ever faw upon a fcull.—Nature, I believe, had a mind by his head to give a proof of her œconomy, not allowing an abundance of thatch to the barn fhe never intended fhould hold any grain.

By

By this time the noife had máde my head ache fo much, that, turning to Scrip, I defired we might make the beft of our way out; which I did with as much joy as ever an infolvent left confinement, and bid adieu to their Bulls, Bears, Scrips, 4 per Cents, and Confolidatings: I had feen and heard enough; and from what I have fince known, am impowered to make the following obfervations.

> The greateft felicity mankind can claim,
> Is to want fenfe of fmart, and be without fenfe
> of fhame.

One would imagine, that the group of Jonathan's Jobbers fat to the poet for this defcription; their infufceptibility, their effrontery, and felf-fufficiency, being too fecure batteries for them ever

ever to be affected by the sharp darts of satire, or galled into such a retrospection of their past life as to imbitter their future days with remorse. It is not the labour in vain of endeavouring to make them *better*, that the author has taken the trouble of drawing up, in a hasty manner, these Anecdotes: No: it is with an honest intent of preventing them from making other people *worse*.

I REMEMBER, under a print of Seymour's representing a horse-dealer shewing his stud to a gentleman, these words are wrote:

"*CAVEAT EMPTOR.*"

THIS is a motto *that* would be extremely proper to be fixed up in large letters at every entrance of Exchange Alley.

A PRETTY

"A pretty fort of a fcoundrel fcribbler this is (obferves Mr. Confolidator). And fo, I fuppofe, this illiterate fellow, becaufe he has no money of his own, would never have any body elfe buy in, and be d—d to him ?"

The term *Job* and *Jobbers* carry an ignominious explanation along with them.

What can be a more contemptible character than a *Beaft-jobber*, a *Horfe-jobber*, or a *Sheep-jobber*,—except a *Stock-jobber* ?

In our auguft Houfe of Parliament, the word *Job* is never made ufe of but to exprefs an action thoroughly bafe : What can be a greater reproach than "to fay, Such a one will undertake any job"—Such a thing is turned into "a job."—Even among the loweft clafs of mankind, is it not a phrafe in common to fay, "I'll do his job?" which fignifies doing him a piece of mifchief fecretly.

YET there is no place, I believe, where the word *Honour* is more frequently ufed than in the Alley. But it is repeated as hypocrites do the word Religion; not for the fake of the thing itfelf, but to ferve their own purpofes. Honour is the mock phrafe for deceit. There is not a proftitute, let her be ever fo abandoned, who will not fwear to you upon her honour; not a Gambler, even the moft notorious, who will not vow to you, he plays upon his honour.

As

A JOURNEY THROUGH LONDON.

As to the GAMBLER and STOCK-JOBBER, not to offend either of thofe remarkable fraternities, the Editor will endeavour, by confidering the merits of each, to fhew how much the two profeffions are analogous.

A GAMBLER is one, who accumulates wealth in contradiction to the known laws of the land, and even in open defiance of them; either by difhonourable combinations, making ufe of falfe dice, or by pretending to be a friend to the perfon whom he intends to plunder, he perfuades his bubble, that he will infure him a certain fafe way of getting a fum of money. This is the cant of thofe who go about the country defrauding the unwary with the game called, *Pricking at the belt.*

Now

Now let us confider, how far any part of this defcription will fuit a common STOCK-JOBBER.

THIS laft mentioned adept in fharping gets money likewife in defiance and contradiction to the laws of the land; and endeavours to take advantage of the credulity of the public, by entering into difhonourable combinations. As the GAMBLER makes ufe of falfe dice, the STOCK-JOBBER makes ufe of falfe intelligences.

SUCH is the fafcinating quality of Gaming, that a fharper fhall be admitted into polite company, although they know he' has no other method of fupporting himfelf than by Gambling; yet their vanity fo far flatters them, that
they

they imagine he muft behave like a man of honour when he plays with *them*.

This, in fome part, is a refemblance of Stock-jobbers, and of the dupes or bubbles who employ them. The Monied Man, or more properly the man who has got fome hundreds beforehand, refembles the farmer whofe hen laid him a golden egg daily; for as the latter, wanting at once to be enriched, ripped up the fowl to get all the wealth without waiting for it; fo he who commences dealer at Jonathan's, would win all at once. He is certain there is a great deal of fharping in the Alley; and that the Jobbers are concerned in it. What then? He has got a Jobber *he* can truft. His Broker won't deceive *him!* *He* is cunning himfelf; *he* can fee—can fee! "It is my
Stock-

Stock-jobber's intereſt to be honeſt to *me:*" *He* has proved that, as plain as noon-day : " He muſt behave upon honour to *me.*"

It is amazing how much the human mind may be deceived by a ſupercilioufneſs of behaviour, and how credulity can be cultivated by cunning. I have myſelf heard an inſolvent in the ſpunging-houſe declare he was ſure the bailiff who arreſted him had a deal of compaſſion for him, and would do any thing for *him*; " be-
" cauſe (continued the unhappy dupe)
" he gave me his word and honour of it."

A GAMBLER may fometimes have an acquaintance, of whom it would be impolitic for him to win money *in propriâ perſonâ*; he has therefore another

other way to take in his very particular friend. He firſt lets him into a ſecret or two at a Race, by which he puts five or ten pieces in his friend's pocket, and next ſhews this very particular friend ſome common tricks at cards, which ſeem to the novice to be great things. The youth, tranſported, dreams of winning an eſtate, thanks his friend the GAMBLER a thouſand and a thouſand times, and ſets out for the Turf, ſure of making his fortune; there, however, by his tutor's contrivances, a brother Gambler is planted, who knowing rather more than the pupil, leaves the would-be ſporting-man without a penny.

I HOPE none of my readers will, at this paſſage, ſhut the book up, and ſay

say with a sigh, or indeed with an oath, "I have been served just so."

Just so do the STOCK-JOBBERS deal with their intimates; for a proof of which, enquire among the Bankrupts who have been rendered so within these last fifteen years in and about London.

To prevent this contagion, if possible, from being universally felt, these pages are written, as also with an endeavour to hinder this nation from being so illegally imposed upon; and the Editor's design will be fully answered, if they shall deter the unexperienced from the absurdest of all infatuations, the imagination that a Jobber will make their fortune, sooner than he will his own.

CHARITY,

CHARITY, it is said, begins at home; and surely the man who is in the secret to attain the nearest road to riches, would rather chuse to travel by himself, than shew a stranger how to take the lead from him.

"Ay, but they have a regard for *me*; it is out of esteem for *my* personal qualities:—I have more money than they to go to market with:—They mustn't be seen in it themselves."

THIS is always the Stock-jobbers cant; and this was the language which the pretenders to the Philosopher's Stone used to bubble their pigeons with.

THE day after we had been at JONA-THAN's, Mr SCRIP called upon me in the morning to acquaint me, that, by

means

means of a Waiter to whom he had formerly been ferviceable, he could let me be an ear-witnefs to a fcene which might divert me: "Becaufe "(continued my friend) there's to be "a fecret meeting of Stock-jobbers "there, and the Waiter has promifed to "place us in the next room, with on- "ly a wainfcot partition between us."

I WENT with him, and we were immediately inducted into a little room, from a peep-hole in the partition of which we could perceive three or four perfons fitting round a large table very well furnifhed with liquor, &c. As I knew Mr. SCRIP could write fhort-hand very dexteroufly, I defired him to take notes of the converfation; which was as follows.

SCENE *the Tavern.*

DRAMATIS PERSONÆ.

SAM DOUBLE-CHIN   TOM TRANSFER
WILL SANSBLUSH   NICK HEMP
PETER PILLORYED   MORDECAI STIVER
BOB TRANSPORT   JERRY SCAMP.

Sam. " Come, gi's a toaft.

Tom. " More friends, and lefs need
" of 'um.

Will. " I fay, let's drink, More fools;
" we have more need of *them*. As to
" friends, let every man be his own
" friend, I fay. I never had any man
" was a friend to me ; and d—n me, if
" I'll be a friend to any man.

Sam. " Come, then, More fools ! 'tis
" Tom's toaft. We fhall like as many
" fools

"fools as Fortune pleases to send us,
"provided they are her favourites,
"and have plenty of the *ready*, or else
"they won't do for us.

Nick. "We won't do for them, you
"mean.

Peter. "We must think of some new
"scheme for this winter, to make peo-
"ple fools, or keep them such. Our
"old pieces of intelligence are grown
"thread-bare; our damn'd fighting ad-
"mirals, and sea fellows, have knock'd
"up all the news about invasions, and
"flat-bottom'd boats; and people,
"now, no more mind whatever para-
"graphs we put in about the French
"preparations, than what's doing at
"the Cape of Good Hope*.

* The reader will remember that this Scene was written in the year 1762.

Sam. "Well, I infift upon it, I con-
"trived the beft hum upon that affair,
"and what anfwered beft for us in the
"Alley, when I fent *Bearsfoot Jack*,
"the fmuggler, to run his floop afhore
"on the Lincolnfhire coaft, and make
"an affidavit before a juftice of peace
"in that county, that the coaft of Bri-
"tany was all lined with troops; that
"there were 40 flat-bottom'd boats
"ready to fail; and that he was cha-
"fed as high as the Humber by three
"French men of war:—and we gave
"him but five guineas for all that.

Jerry. "Before that news came,
"ftocks were done at $84\frac{5}{8}$, and they
"fell next day to $69\frac{1}{8}$; you know we
"all wanted to buy in then.

Will. "But what fignifies jawing
"about what has been done? We know
"that

"that well enough; we all tafted the
"fweets of that, and only wifh we
"cou'd do fo again.

Peter. "We muft do fo, or fomething
"like it. We muft keep the ftocks
"down this winter, if we can; they'll
"rife of themfelves, I'm fure; there-
"fore down we muft have them, or
"there will be no dealings for us.

Nick. "Why, here's Mordecai writes
"the Dutch letters, don't he? and
"there's Tom Tranfport writes the
"French ones, that come round by
"Holland, to tell them what they
"fhall fay.

Mor. "As I fall fay, gentlemans,
"by mine zole, de people here are zo
"zlym as de devil. By Got Almoyty,
"dere is no more but as de dicknefs of
"a zeet

"a zeet of paber between de cun-
"ning of de Englifh and our own peo-
"ple.

Tom. "Why, then, we muft out-cun-
"ning them, muftn't we, Old Swine's-
"face?

Mor. "Yaw, wid aw mine art.

Sam. "This affair of Ruffia will af-
"ford us fine matter for intelligence.—
"We can depofe the Emprefs Regent,
"and raife a rebellion there—that will
"do for one day;—and we can fay fhe
"has declared war againft the King of
"Pruffia—that's another;—or give it
"out fhe has put our minifter under an
"arreft—that will do for another.

Bob. "But where's our wafte-book?
"Why don't we enter thefe intelligen-
"ces

"ces down?—Let's see now, for Octo-
"ber, people begin to come to town:
"very inquisitive about news.

Will. "Yes, but then they have no mo-
"ney in their pockets; they have been
"stock-jobbing all their loose corns
"at horse-racing, and high-gammer
"cocks.

Tom. "What the devil's high-gammer
"cocks? Greek?

Will. "Greek!—Well, if I am an Irish-
"man, what then? I suppose being a
"Grecian's as good as being an En-
"glishman, at any time. I a'n't
"asham'd of my country: I wasn't
"sent out of it; no, I came out of it on
"my own accord.

Tom.

Tom. " Yes, becaufe you cou'dn't
" ftay any longer in it. What was
" that your landlady mifs'd out of her
" lodgings, when you made your efcape
" at Cork from the conftable?

Will. " Here's a pretty fellow to
" talk about lodgings!—Don't you
" remember the time you had not one?
" Wasn't you bred up under Covent-
" garden herb-ftalls; and wasn't the
" firft houfe you ever flept in, the
" Round-houfe, which you was put into
" upon fufpicion?

Peter. " Gentlemen, I can perceive
" you are both to blame.

Tom. " You can perceive! Good
" Lord, good Lord! I fuppofe you
" can't perceive as much now, as you
" did

"did one day, fome years ago, when
"you was exalted as Overfeer of the
"Haymarket, juft by way of an exhibi-
"tion. Who performed fo dextroufly
"at the Opera-houfe one mafquerade-
"night, in contriving fome odd fort of
"Passages?.

Sam. "D——n all thefe difputes, what
"fignifies what we were? And as to
"what we have done, I don't fuppofe
"honefty ever had much dealings with
"many of us. We can get money if
"we will, and let us but do that, and
"who'll fay any thing againft us? fo let
"us fettle intelligence for the enfuing
"winter.

Nick. "October—You know, now
"the people in general come from the
"country very healthy, and therefore
"will

"   will be more frighted about sickness,
" as the more money a man has,
" the more unwilling he is to part
" with it. So, suppose we have a
" plague broke out at Leghorn; it is a
" bad time of year, indeed; however,
" they won't think of that, and it will
" terrify damnably.

Sam. " But how will this best be done?

Nick. " Why, *Bearsfoot* is at Lisbon
" now, you know; and I'll send him
" instructions how he shall dispatch
" four or five letters over to England,
" and where they shall be planted.

Bob. " Well; but mustn't we have
" some quarrels puff'd to have happen-
" ed among the Ministry?

Sam.

Sam. "It is time enough for that;
" and then, you know, we have three
" special hands to take all that trouble
" upon themselves. I'll hold ten pound
" to one, they are the three best peo-
" ple for court scandal, and court intel-
" ligence, that can be. There's Bet,
" that my Lord Thing-o'-me keeps;
" and the Waiter at What-d'ye-call-
" um's; and Sir Thomas's valet de
" chambre; it is only giving them a
" hint who we want to be whispered is
" to be in, or to be out; and I'll be
" d——d if they won't spread the news
" about so circumstantially, and seem-
" ingly so well authenticated, that they
" would almost make infidels believe
" it.

Jerry. "Very well, we have news
" enough for October; then comes No-
" vember and December.

Nick.

Nick. "O, they are hanging and
" drowning months! Any thing will
" do then that is but dreadful; an
" earthquake, or an invasion.

Bob. " I say, an invasion won't do.

Sam " Our best plan this winter
" will be to play off a " Peace, or No
" peace"——that's a scheme which
" mayn't happen again a great while;
" and let all our other hums alone for
" the present, they'll be new against
" another time; so enter " Peace or No
" peace" into our book, and let's begin
" to prepare proper intelligence accor-
" dingly.

Will. " But don't you think we may
" puff off Denmark's declaring war
" against Russia, or Russia against Den-
" mark?

" mark ? Or suppose we kill the King
" of Prussia by a conspiracy, one post;
" and bring him to life again the next,
" eh ?

Bob. " Those are things of course.

Jerry. " Well then, I'll tell you
" what we'll do. Here are eight of us;
" we'll divide four and four, half for
" a peace, half against it. You four
" shall mark us out your men; we four
" will mark you out ours as employ us.
" We'll either fill them full of hopes,
" or frighten them out of their wits;
" you must do just the same; so then
" they'll be between hawk and buzzard,
" hoping and despairing, selling out,
" buying in; and the commission-mo-
" ney all here, all here, boys! And it
" can't look, you know, as if we had
" any

"any intereft in it; becaufe, you know, we don't advife thofe people who we deal for.

Omnes. "Right, right! Come, drink fuccefs to the fcheme.—Come, bufinefs is fettled, fo now for pleafure. Agreed, agreed."

AFTER we had left the company at the tavern, and were croffing Lincolns-Inn Fields, we were obliged to pafs a great mob; when afking one of the by-ftanders what the matter was, he informed us that a couple of people had been fighting there ——— But I fhall give the affair in the man's own words, or as nearly as I can.

"You muft know, Gentlemen, as how that there man there that goes along

"along there is a pick-pocket, and fo
"indeed is his friend he has been fight-
"ing with. They fell out here about
"finding fault with one another, for
"not dealing upon honour, as they
"fhould have done. Becaufe you muft
"know, Sir, that one of 'um fold the
"other man's fifter, who deals in caft
"cloaths, twelve white handkerchiefs,
"or flower'd ones, to be deliver'd laft
"fpring, the fecond week *Ranelor*
"open'd, at fuch a price. Well, he did
"fo. But the other went to his friend's
"mother's ftall, (fhe has one in **Rag-**
"**fair**) and fold her twelve filk hand-
"kerchiefs at fuch a price to be deli-
"ver'd a week after the Playhoufes
"open'd, and got a crown earneft; and
"now he won't be as good as his word;
"and fo the other beat him for it, and
"told us the whole ftory."

"I ASKED

I asked the man, if thefe fellows openly declared themfelves to be pickpockets; and if they did fo, why had not fome perfon feiz'd them?

" Lord help you, Sir! (his reply
" was) Why, who do you think wou'd
" take them here? Why, Sir, a pick-
" pocket is as fafe here, Sir, as—as—"

" Ay, (replied Mr. Scrip) as a
" Stock-jobber at Jonathan's. As to
" the fellow that would not deliver the
" handkerchiefs, and refufed to fulfil
" his contract, he is a Lame Duck.

This being a phrafe I never heard before, I defired my friend to explain it to me, which, as foon as we were at home, he did in the following manner.

" A Lame

"A Lame Duck, Sir, is a man who in 'Change-Alley has committed the very same action, in respect of selling for time, as this fellow has done, who was just now beat by his brother rogue.

"Every year, Sir, there are people who make bargains for large quantity of stock; either subscribe for it to one of the Government's Loans, or else sell it for time; depending, before the day of payment comes, that things will turn out in their favour; or, in other words, they toss up so much money of another person's against—nothing of their own; for they at the time of making these bargains are perhaps worse than nothing. If they are out of luck, and have the turn against
"them,

" them, they refuse to fulfil their con-
" tract, and waddle away with the title
" of LAME DUCKS."

" BUT what punishment attends them
" for such behaviour?"

" THEY are deny'd the privilege of
" coming into JONATHAN's for about
" six weeks, although they have liber-
" ty to trade in the Alley as usual, and
" are no more affected with this igno-
" miny, than a common strumpet
" would be, who is surprised with a
" man bed-fellow in her arms.

" BUT, Sir, this behaviour is yet
" more shocking, if considered as it
" ought to be, than perhaps it may ap-
" pear to you at first fight.— While I
" was entangled in the Alley, I sold
" one

" one of the *Family* ten thoufand pounds
" of ftock for time. I loft 1050 l. by
" it, and when his bargain became due,
" I paid him the difference, 1050 l. in
" Bank bills. In lefs than fix weeks
" afterwards, I bought 12,000 l. of
" him for time. The event turning
" out in my favour, I was to have re-
" ceived of him 1675 l. but he refus'd
" to fulfil his contract, would not givè
" me fix-pence, and went a Lame Duck
" out of the Coffee-houfe; and this is
" all the fatisfaction I ever could get.

" Now would I be glad to hear any
" impartial perfon's opinion concerning
" fuch people; and whether the fellow
" who ftops a ftage-coach, and openly
" ventures his life againft the chance of
" getting perhaps not above a guinea
" or two, is not the honefter man.—But
                                              " I can

"I can hardly keep my temper, while
"I am talking on this subject: the
"wrongs I have received, the iniqui-
"ties which are every day practised, and
"practised with impunity by that par-
"ticular set of people — God is good,
"to be sure; too good for some folks,
"I fancy; else Providence would have
"called them forth to publick justice
"before this time: or perhaps I com-
"mit a sin in saying that Providence
"befriends them — Their deeds are
"infernal, I am certain; certainly there-
"fore Satan shields his liege subjects.

"When there were public gaming-
"houses in London, and Hazard play'd
"at openly, there was a man who used
"to frequent them all, and make betts
"with every one who did not know him,
"from five shillings to five guineas;

"it

" it was all the fame to him, he had
" no cafh. If he won, he received the
" money; if he loft, he knew the con-
" fequence, he muft undergo a kick-
" ing; and he ftood that as well as
" any LAME DUCK does denying to ful-
" fil his contract.—This at Hazard-
" table is called LEVANTING.

" Now if fuch a difcipline was to be
" put in practice among the LEVAN-
" TERS at Jonathan's—fuppofe every
" LAME DUCK was to be foot-ball'd
" up and down the walks of the Change,
" three or four times on each walk,
" then kick'd over the area, for about
" ten minutes, between the hours of
" one and two in the middle of any
" day in the week, Sunday excepted; it
" would not only be very beneficial ex-
" ercife for the health of the gentlemen
" upon

"upon 'Change, but keep other peo-
"ple's principles in good order, and
"might have as fine an effect upon the
"'Change-Alley dealers, as feeing the
"play of George Barnwell has had
"upon feveral London 'prentices."

It was noon the next day before I faw Mr. Scrip, who appearing to be very chearful, I congratulated him upon it. He told me, that the phyficians had that morning pronounced his wife to be recovered; and that fhe was to be removed as foon as he could get an apartment ready for her. That bufinefs I defired him to make himfelf perfectly eafy about, fince my fifter, who was fingle, and one who Mrs. Scrip had often vifited, " infifted upon his wife's
" coming down into the country to
' her immediately upon her recovery,
"to

"to reſtore her intirely." Theſe were the words of her letter, which I ſhew'd him: it was an anſwer to one I had written to my ſiſter, with an account of the diſtreſſes of her former acquaintance.

My friend's eyes were tear-full as he read the letter; and when he returned it, he was beginning, with a heart almoſt burſting with gratitude, to acknowledge the favour, as he called it: but his eagerneſs to explain what he felt on my ſiſter's expreſſing herſelf ſo tenderly for his wife's health, rendered him incapable of uttering intelligibly what he meant to ſay.

I stopped him from going on, and inſiſted, if he valued my friendſhip, that he would never mention a word more of any ſervice that might be rendered him

him either by myself or my sister; and, in order to give him time to recover himself, I took a walk in the garden.

The satisfaction which the human mind receives when it beholds a fellow-creature happy, especially if the spectator has any way contributed to the peace or pleasure of that person, is so exquisite a heart-felt gratification, that I wonder the multitude of pleasure-hunters, who expend such vast sums in endeavouring to make themselves happy, will ever employ themselves in any other action. It is a refinement upon pleasure, a rectified felicity, which satiety can never reach, nor the terrors of approaching old age ever appal.

For a moment, I must own, I was a little vain, on considering myself contrafted with thofe wretches who had ruined Mr. Scrip. As my fortune enabled me to carry my defign into execution, I was determined to affift him with fuch a pecuniary loan as would enable him to enter into bufinefs again with reputation and credit.

The thought gave me great pleafure; I dwelt indeed for fome time upon the reflection; and could not help thinking, that if even the intention of doing right afforded the mind an agreeable fenfation, certainly the commiffion of wrong muft be attended with horror, fome time or other, to the infamous perpetrators.

How much farther may we extend the profpect between the rewards of virtue and villainy, if we will reflect upon an Hereafter! A right-thinking mind,

mind, by that prospect, is fortified to endure

> The whips and scorns of Time,
> The oppressor's wrongs, the proud man's contumely;

to labour for his little family along life's rugged road, bearing at the same time the heavy burthen of necessity. Yet that reflection lightens his load, unfolding to him that glorious tho' distant view of an eternal beatitude, prepared by the Almighty for those who love him, and keep his commandments.

YET even this hope, this promise of futurity, would not be entirely satisfactory to some minds, unless they were assured that there are punishments as well as rewards; and that the Extortioners, the Stock-jobbers, with the rest of the Vice-raised Unworthies, shall be snatched from their ill-obtain'd splendors, and hurled howling into irredeemable perdition.

By this time I supposed Mr. SCRIP had pretty well recovered himself, and on my return we agreed to dine together at the tavern. Just as we were going out, we met my sister, who was come to Town on purpose to see my friend's wife; and if Mrs. SCRIP was well enough, she told us, she would take her down the next day into the country with her.

In consequence of my sister's arrival, we attended her to BEDLAM.

When we arrived at the Hospital, I could not help admiring those two figures placed over the entrance, representing

senting Melancholy Madnefs, and Ravings. But common-place praifes are fo eafy to make, and the terms of art fo hackney'd, that I forbear any eulogium on thofe pieces of fculpture, left it may be thought, I only extol them to exhibit my own capacity as a connoiffeur.

YET it is pity fo little care has been taken of two fuch excellent figures, that we have neither cafts, models, nor drawings of them *. Expofed to the weather, they are decaying; and no more attended to than the weather-beaten roof of a country cottage.

* This complaint has been fince removed, by an elegant Engraving of both being prefixed to an account of this excellent Inftitution, written by the Rev. Mr. BOWEN, at the requeft of the Governors, at whofe expence it was alfo printed, and diftributed.   EDIT.

It is not, indeed, to be expected, that immensely polite personages should admire such figures : the subjects are too shocking for the extreme delicacy of the present taste ; although ladies permit Chinese monsters and pot-bellied Mandarins to be placed in their apartments. But those are foreign figures, and therefore must be vastly entertaining; while such English frights as madmen, and made at home too, must be horridly shocking, and vastly low.

Another reason why these excellent pieces of statuary are not more famous, is, they are put up in a part of the Town which is never visited by any of the *Connoisseur, Dilettanti,* or *Virtuosi,* Clubs, without (as is very often the case) those gentlemen critics are brought there as lodgers.

Neither

Neither can they be often mentioned at great men's tables, becaufe no artift ever publifhed any book about them, to point out their feveral beauties; wherefore the elocutionifts and dabblers in the arts and fciences (who are fo eager to fhew their tafteful talents, and harangue upon the merits of the ancient and demerits of the modern artifts, and fo elaborately run on from the fhafts of the columns of Balbeck to the flutings of a North-country cockle-fhell) for want of being taught what to fay, and not having any books to ftudy their parts, are forced to be mute; moft modern profeffors of tafte being only parroted into judgment; and repeat their leffons as poor catholics do their Pater-Nofter, without underftanding the words they utter..

When.

When we entered Bedlam, it was impossible for us not to feel a momentary sorrow for the different objects we saw around, " who seemed to shew va-
" riety of wretchedness."

But on an examination of these people, whom vulgar error stigmatizes as *unhappy* Lunatics, we found it a false prejudice to call them unhappy; it is only those who are in a state of rationality that can possibly be pronounced miserable.

We are the unhappy beings; tame animals, trusted to run about the streets, because we are supposed to carry a guide along with us called Reason, who, like a lamp-light in a prison, has just force enough to expose the horror around us.

Doubts,

Doubts, disappointments, mortifications, and the whole train of the mind's miseries, Reason is the occasion of our enduring; while the more happy Lunatics have no such sensations. Deck'd out with their straw, they dance and sing,

" That a madman can be
" More a monarch than he, than he, " &c.

To the ballad-makers to the Opera and the Theatres-Royal, I recommend a tour now and then to Bedlam; where they may furnish themselves with hints for dresses, grotesque figures, and droll attitudes; for several patients of the Hospital are exquisitely happy in fancying their straw, and have great variety of steps, as well as distortions.

AND I humbly recommend their tafte to the infpection of the prefent *Fafhion-fanciers*; for it is prefumed that Folly's wardrobe muft be pretty well exhaufted, and there is now no other genius to depend upon for the Town's tafte but *Lunacy*, *Folly*'s younger fifter.

PERHAPS, compaffionate reader, thou may'ft blame me for attempting to treat a fubject of this nature ludicroufly. Thou may'ft fuppofe, that mad people are too wretched a fet of beings for any man who has feeling about him, to aim at being droll upon.

I DO not mean to make merry with their misfortunes; God forbid I fhould! but we too often mifplace our compaf- fion: we feel more for them, than they

do

do for themselves; we mistake both their cases, and our own; nay, we are too apt to mix pride with our pity, and compare their wretchedness to our own affluence, and then exult, reflecting on that false superiority.

THESE Lunatics are locked up, because they would be what they are not. But what should we do for mad-houses, if all the men and women out of Bedlam were to be confined, that are at this present writing infected with the same light-headedness — of appearing what they are not?

WHAT are envy, insolence, meanness, scandal, conceit, and a million more of diseases that distemper the human mind, but so many stages of madness?

Are

Are we not in general a set of ill-natured, restless existences, who always hurry after pleasure, but ever run ourselves out of breath before we reach it? or else a set of selfish, incurious beings, whose whole minds are tainted by the fever of avarice, or the rust of indolence?

Let us take a review of the bulk of human kind, and consider what composes the multitude, but an aggregate of pretenders and dupes, who become so by the villainy of others, or their own vanity.

In the first room, or cell, we came to in Bedlam, was a merry lodger singing a medley song about "Drink and "drive care away"— " Wine does " wonders every day"—and " Sing tan-
" tararara

"tararara brave fport."—He call'd out to us to give him a toaft.—This man, we found on enquiry, had been a very famous Choice Spirit, who drank himfelf into a fever, which fettling in the weakeft or moft impair'd part about him, viz. his head, reduced him to the condition in which we faw him. He invited us to Comus' Court; told us the Devil was to be in the chair; and that there would be hellifh high fun there.

In the middle of the floor or way, as we walked up and down the ward, there were three or four patients playing at chuck with halfpence. Thefe I took to be gamblers; but the keeper we had with us declared that he knew them all before they came in, and that they never gamed in their life-times until they loft their fenfes.

I EN-

I ENQUIRED of him, if they ever had any gamblers confined as Lunatics.— " No, Sir, (replied he) they fend us a " great many madmen, but are never " mad enough to come here themfelves, " except one, and we were forced to " turn him out of the houfe; for when " he got well enough to be allowed the " liberty of walking up and down the " wards, he ufed to pick people's poc- " kets of their handkerchiefs, as he pre- " tended to fhew them the houfe."

ACROSS us ftalk'd a man who had no other covering than a blanket, neither would he wear any other; " becaufe " (as he told us) Adam was cloath'd in " flefh, but for himfelf he was a Pre- " adamite."

I TOLD

I TOLD our guide this man was too mad to be trufted loofe.—" Ah, dear Sir ! " (he replied, fhaking his head) Why, " Sir, there are feveral people fo fond of " his doctrine, that we fhould lofe ta- " king pounds if we were to fhut him " up. Sir, there are feveral females " come to him to be converted ; and we " are apt to believe that his doctrine is " like a chapel of eafe to Methodifm.

I THEN felt myfelf plucked by the fleeve ; and turning about, faw a little figure at my elbow, with a very ordinary waiftcoat on, a flannel night-cap, and a beard about half a year's growth, who begged I wou'd give him fome tobacco, and he would communicate fome fecrets to us.-

Ac-

ACCORDINGLY we followed him into his room; where he told us, that the Government had confined him there, because he would not difcover to them the fecret of making gold; " for, gentle-
" men, I have the Philofopher's Stone.
" You may talk of your Pay-mafters,
" and your Army and Navy Contrac-
" tors, Commiffaries or Stock-jobbers,
" having the grand magifterium, they
" have not; 'tis only wheels within
" wheels with them.—Mine is the
" *opus operatum* only.——However,
" my Country is ungrateful, the fecret
" fhall die with me; but I like you,
" and I'll make your fortunes, by gi-
" ving you fome other noftrums."

OUT of a deal-box he pulled feveral parcels, and giving me one, told me, it was an elixir drawn from cobwebs to cure eure squinting; that Mr. JACOB HENRIQUES had promised him to solicit a patent for him; but the only objection made against it was, that people now-a-days were not to look straight forwards.

THEN he gave me a phial, which he said " was the essence of charcoal, and " a great specific to prevent hair turn- " ing grey; and to cure the Gout, Le- " prosy, and Palsy."

WE took our leaves of him; and assured him we were highly obliged to him.

THE confining of this secret-maker was, I thought, a loss to the world; because his nostrums might be, and very pobably were, as good in their kind, as

any

any other of the prefent advertifed uni-
verfal medicines.

EVERY Toyfhop is turned into a Dif-
penfary, and every Chandler's fhop diftri-
butes medicines for all forts of difeafes;
and while the fquabble of party prevents
our fuperiors from attending to thofe
empiricks, thefe advertifing quacks
poifon whole parifhes with impunity.

THE Bedlam doctor, as a madman,
fancied he was right in what he did, and
acted uniformly from that fancy: but
what name can we give to thofe who
purchafe *Elixirs, Jefuits Drops, Greek
Water, Lotions, Innocent Compounds*, and
feveral more obnoxious preparations?

ALL the difference between his
drugs and theirs is, that in BEDLAM it is
a mad-

a madman who has made the compofitions; while the makers of thofe which are fold without, are in their fenfes; it is only the buyers who are Lunatics.

AT our return from Moorfields, I was agreeably furprifed to find Mrs. SCRIP there, and in a tranquility of mind I could not have expected. And I wifh every *wit*, every *fine gentleman*, and all the other fet of felf-fufficient beings, who think it fo extremely advantageous to their reprefentations to be continually ridiculing marriage, and condemning the tender, the delicate fentiments which wives can fo amiably exprefs, had but been witnefs to the behaviour of my friend's wife.

Not a syllable of reproach escaped her for all which she had suffered from the indiscretions of her husband; not one sorrowful retrospection, on her side, of what she had been: no, on the contrary, she comforted her husband, and bade him rely on that Providence which had already so unexpectedly relieved them from the depth of misery. Then she gratefully addressed herself to us; and while she was thus charming us all, with that delicacy which, though it is impossible to describe, is so easy for true politeness to use, I could not help thinking how contemptible our school declamations were of Pedantic Philosophy! how insipid our coffee-house political harangues for national or notional good! What were they to one half hour of a fine tender sensible woman's conversation!

fation! what all our tavern repartees, jollities, common-place ftories, fentiments, or betts-making! I grew afhamed of myfelf, and of my fex; and was compelled, fpite of pride, to acknowledge, THAT NATURE'S NICEST ACCOMPLISHMENTS BELONG NOT TO THE MALE, BUT FEMALE PART OF HUMAN KIND.

WHILE I was indulging myfelf with one of the moft amiable family-pictures I ever faw; which was, the regard this lately fo very an unhappy couple paid each to the other; a Clergyman, an intimate and old acquaintance of mine, fent a card defiring to fpeak to me immediately.

I WAITED on him at the coffee-houfe mentioned in his note; when he told

me,

me, that he had troubled me to enquire concerning Mr. and Mrs. Scrip, as a valuable eftate had fallen to them, by the fudden deaths of the three fucceeding heirs.

I IMMEDIATELY informed him of their ftory.—We thought it not proper to acquaint them at once with their fudden good fortune : by degrees, however, we let them know how happy they were in refpect to circumftances; and in a very few days afterwards they fet out for the country to take poffeffion of their eftate, and where I have fince had the heart-elating fatisfaction to fee them in a ftate of unaffected tranquility. To me this proved an inexpreffible pleafure. What more can delight the human mind, than to fee worthy objects of his own fpecies happy! Are

25 per

25 per cent. accumulations capable of bringing home such joy to the heart? Statesmen, Pensioners, and Favourites, what say you? Unknown to ye all are such social enjoyments; for, contrary to the received maxims of what the world may hold, ye live not for yourselves; and yet at the same time cannot enjoy pleasure from what you do to others; because you are conscious that it is INTEREST, and not ESTEEM, which buys and sells between you.

THUS far my speculations on the Metropolis had afforded me little pleasure. —My affection for mankind was hourly diminishing as my knowledge increased. —I saw knaves batten on the spoils of the honest but ignorant, and hardly cover their villainy with the thin threadbare veil of hypocrify.—Hitherto I had hoped, from a diligent examination into my own bofom, that the invectives I had read in books againft the depravity of the human heart, were, if not unfounded, at leaft extremely exaggerated; but I confefs this prefumption was weakened, and the Hiftory of Mr. Scrip almoft entirely demolifhed my good opinion and reverence for my fpecies.

Yet, perhaps, thought I, his particular loffes may have foured his temper, and the difappointment of his hopes diftorted his imagination and warped his judgment.—It is not, at any rate, from the fraudulent machinations of thofe unrighteous fons of Mammon whom he defcribed, that we are

to

to eftimate the general morality of this great City; out of that noxious atmofphere, fit only for the refpiration of fuch monfters, I may ftill fi..d generofity and honour among the men, delicacy and tendernefs among the women. —I will not at once refign the opinion which for five-and-twenty years I have entertained of human nature. To-morrow I will return to my friend FLIGHT, communicate thofe obfervations which have ftruck me, and take his opinion on all I have yet feen.

FULL of thefe thoughts I was juft fetting out to my friend, when I received a letter from a Nobleman who honoured me with his patronage, informing me that the Incumbent of a living of 600l. a year, in his gift, was deceafed; that he propofed me as the

the succeffor; and that the earlier I went down to be inducted into it the better.

Though this summons of course put an immediate stop to my further residence and speculation in London, it did not prevent my calling, as I had intended, on my friend Flight, to whom I communicated the news, which he received with great pleasure.—" How-
" ever," said he, " though you cannot
" now stay to view every thing here
" with your own eyes, it is in my
" power to furnish you with a Picture
" of the Metropolis, of which I will
" venture to assure you there is not
" one feature exaggerated."

Then going to his desk he took out a manuscript: " This," added he,
" contains the Memoirs of one of
" the

"the unfortunate DAUGHTERS OF PLEA-
"SURE, as they are miscalled; of those
"wretched women, I mean, who pro-
"stitute their charms for a miserable
"subsistence. It was put into my hands
"by the Man whom you observed (when
"you were last here and paid a visit with
"me to the COLONEL above stairs) to
"sit in a very melancholy posture,
"and who is as different in aspect as he
"is in manners and principles from the
"riotous, noisy, and unthinking com-
"pany we then abruptly quitted in so
"much confusion.

"THERE is something very extraor-
"dinary, Mr. SPECULIST," (continued
FLIGHT) "in the story of that man.
"His daughter was one of the hand-
"somest and vainest girls living. Her
"father, like your friend SCRIP, was
"in-

" infatuated with 'Change-Alley; and,
" from being a wealthy tradesman,
" soon became an indigent debtor, and
" was arrested for 500l. by a man of
" fortune, who pretended the utmost
" friendship for him, but who was
" one of the basest libertines that
" ever disgraced human appearance.
" The beauty of the daughter made
" him determine upon the ruin of the
" father, that he might be sure to
" have Miss on his own terms, falling at
" once from extreme gaiety to extreme
" poverty. He has been in prison these
" eight years, during which time his
" daughter has been, as the phrase is,
" *upon the Town*, and in that profession
" has experienced all its dreadful varie-
" ties, according to her own Narrative,
" which I have had to correct for her;
" and which, as I believe you can do it
" better

" better than I can, I will lend you to
" look over. The adventures are ge-
" nuine, the scenes real, and the ob-
" fervations juft.—They will furnifh
" an excellent fequel to what you
" have yourfelf feen, and from both
" you may form an authentic and
" founded opinion of the moral depra-
" vity of mankind.— Farewel, my
" friend! I wifh you all manner of
" profperity. Whenever your affairs
" call you again to London, you will
" probably find me here; for I am
" convinced, from the inhumanity of
" fome of my creditors, that unlefs the
" Legiflature fhould humanely inter-
" pofe in my favour, my confine-
" ment will probably be for life."

I WAS pained by the fight of poor FLIGHT's diftrefs, which I endeavoured to alleviate by a Bank note, and which I promifed to repeat annually: then fhaking him by the hand, I told him that I received his propofal with pleafure, as I thought there might be fomething inftructive, and confequently worthy of communication to the Public in the Life of a Kept-Miftrefs. I accordingly put the manufcript in my pocket, with which, on perufal, I was fo well pleafed, that I fhall prefent it without further ceremony as the fequel to my intended JOURNEY THROUGH LONDON.

AUTHEN-

AUTHENTIC LIFE

OF A

WOMAN of the TOWN.

Ah ! what avails how once appear'd the fair,
   When from gay equipage she falls obscure ;
In vain she moves her livid lips in pray'r,
   What man so mean to recollect the poor ?
From place to place, by unfee'd bailiffs drove,
   As fainting fauns from thirsty blood-hounds
     fly ;
See the sad remnants of unhallow'd love
   In prisons perish, or on dunghills die.
Pimps and dependants once her beauties prais'd ;
   And on those beauties, vermin-like, they fed ;
From wretchedness, the crew her bounty rais'd,
   When by her spoils enrich'd, deny her bread.
Thro' street to street she wends, as want betides,
   Like *Shore's* sad wife in winter's dismal hours ;
The bleak winds piercing her unnourish'd sides,
   Her houseless head dripping with drizzly
     showers.

Sickly she strolls amidst the miry lane,
  While streaming spouts dash on her uncloath'd
    neck;
By famine pin'd, pinch'd by disease-bred pain,
  Contrition's portrait, and rash Beauty's wreck,
She dies, sad outcast! heart-broke by remorse;
  Pale stretch'd against th' inhospitable doors;
While gathering gossips taunt the fleshless corse,
  And thank their Gods, *that they were never whores.*

SHOULD I begin this Narrative with a penitential preface, to supplicate, to implore the compassion of my readers, according to the common introductory method of those novels which have been written concerning us unhappy women, I should give the lye to my mind, for I want not the world's pity.

WHEN I begged for mercy, 'twas denied me; when I merited compassion,
I met

I met with contempt; and when I deserved reproach, received adoration.

My own sex treated me like an enemy, mankind used me as a slave.—At first I fancied myself beloved by them: they presented, they knelt, they swore themselves to be my admirers; but before I had commenced Kept-Mistress a year, I discovered enough of that sex to make me despise them; and the principal design of this Narrative is, to exhibit mankind as they are, as they behave in their connections with our sex; among that part of it, I mean, whom they either find abandoned, or make so.

It is not to indulge a splenetic fit for former ill-treatment that I write—I am not angry with either sex. With respect to my own, their vanity is their punishment;

ment. As to the other sex, indeed, I have been used ill by them; but circumstances and time gave me opportunities to revenge my wrongs.

To you, ye Men, ye self-supposed Lords, and Prerogative-makers, to you this Narrative is addressed; not so much to make you know yourselves, as to make you remember yourselves. Conscious of what most of you are, most of you I must despise.—The *Abject*, the *Ideot*, the *Madman*, the *Villain*, the *Sharper*, the *Sycophant*, the *Bully*, are characters which every MAN personates in turn, who is mean enough to attempt at possession by deceit.

MY father was a very reputable tradesman in the city of London. He married a Clergyman's daughter, who was remarkably handsome, and had an ex-

treme

treme good education, but not one shilling of fortune.

As she had not only been brought up to dance, sing and play, visit, and be one of the first in every fashion or diversion; my father, who was the most indulgent husband living, gave her the same liberty she had enjoyed before marriage; and as soon as I was old enough, I was allowed to take her for my pattern.

I WAS kept at a Boarding-school until twelve years of age, and learnt there from the conversation of my companions, in two or three months, things which would astonish my readers should I relate them. Persons who never were within those seminaries cannot conceive that girls just entering into their Teens, could be such minute natural philosophers, in ideas at least, as we were.

I GREW

I GREW very womanish, as I was told, and was proud of hearing it, as all girls are; and even when I was but juſt Thirteen, took the Woman very much upon me, in behaving as I ſaw ladies behave. My mother uſed to ſay, that nothing was ſo proper to bring any young perſon forward as letting them ſee the World, and come early into company. I paid and received viſits, had billet-doux ſent me, returned anſwers, and made parties among young perſons of both ſexes about my own age. But to this day, experienced as I have been, and almoſt by hackney uſe above or beneath bluſhing at indelicacies, I cannot help wondering, I ſay (even now), what then paſſed amongſt us; and I dare avow, that permitting girls and boys from eleven to thirteen to be together as play-mates, may be productive of of habits, or confequences, which are better to be imagined than expreffed.

For the probability of this affertion, I appeal to the remembrance of moft of my readers.

My conftitution was one of the moft fanguine. In high health and great fpirits, praifed for my figure, at thirteen years of age fuppofed to be fifteen, (fo much was I grown) I began to be horridly uneafy at the leaft reftraint—I wanted to be unbounded in my gratifications—I would have every momentary wifh inftantly gratified.—Nothing but an irrefolution of being incapable where to fix, prevented my afking many a fine-dreffed fellow to go off with me.— But thofe wifhes were on reflection curbed,

curbed, I grew afhamed of myfelf, and vowed that I would wait with patience.

Then I heard moft melancholy and moft difmal accounts, (which my father being Churchwarden made to be oftener talked of) how wretchedly a poor ftreet-walker died upon a bulk, or was fent to Bridewell half-naked to be whipped; and thefe events always concluded with one obfervation, That all whores muft come to the fame end.

Shocked at thefe relations, I ufed to retire often to my chamber and cry; vow I never would be abandoned, never be a ftrumpet; and yet in ten minutes a fudden glow of defire filled my mind, and I was all-frantic for poffeffion; efpecially when I obferved women whom both my father and mother

knew

knew to be proftitutes, to ftop at our door in their own equipages; and then, when I faw the refpect paid them, I fuppofed that the terrible ftories I had heard were only invented to frighten me, and therefore determined to be one, as gay, and as happy, as the moft famous woman of pleafure upon the town.

Big with my irregular fcheme, I indulged, I enjoyed it in contemplation, and only waited to felect from my admirers the man whom I could moft fancy, being determined to confent on his firft propofal to go off with him.

This intention, however, was rendered abortive by the praifes which my mother was continually pouring upon me. She affured me, that a young perfon of my accomplifhments, and of my

ap-

appearance, might be very certain, if she would but have a common share of prudence and patience, to marry a nobleman. A coronet on my post-chariot, —the flambeaux blazing before my chair on a Birth-night—the title--the—a thousand and a thousand dreams of grandeur rose at once in my mind; I found myself to be certainly formed for a woman of quality; believed I should be so; and immediately determined to bury the thoughts of every irregular scheme.

My vanity this time saved me from becoming abandoned, and I experienced the truth of what Archer says,

Pride saves man oft, and woman too, from falling.

But, conscious of the warmth of my
con-

conftitution, I would not truft myfelf on any private parties of pleafure for the future, left one unlucky moment fhould put an end to all my future hopes of extreme fplendor.

I WOULD not accept of one invitation, unlefs my mother was of the party; I would not truft myfelf out of her fight, nor ever fuffer any gentleman even to kifs my hand, unlefs there was a glove on it. Thefe felf-denials gave me inexpreffible pain; but what will not a Woman, when fhe has refolved on any meafure, fuffer? Man's refolution is no more to compare to our's for ftrength, than wafer-paper to heart of oak.

THIS behaviour occafioned me to be praifed by every father and mother where I vifited, and my example was

pro-

propofed as a pattern for their daughters. I was extolled as the very emblem of chaftity, at the inftant my veins burnt with the fever of voluptuoufnefs.—But thus is the world deceived by appearances. I, who had not the merit of the leaft virtue, was looked upon as the moft virtuous : yet fo it is, reputations are too often gained, not by really being, but only by feeming to be.

TORTURED as I was by appetite, I determined to become a martyr to my defires, rather than forego this fcheme of a quality-marriage. Every day I expected the happy moment when through the fafh I fhould fee the coroneted chariot ftop at our door, and the gay ftar-breafted Peer ftep out, to afk my parents confent to lead me to the altar.

I WENT

I went to York with my mother on a visit to a relation; and during the races, I appeared there the reigning toast. Among others, Lord L——behaved to me in so particular a manner, and addressed me so tenderly, so respectfully, that I had no doubt but he was the nobleman who was to fulful my parents predictions.

That very person, however, that man of mighty honours, has since confessed to me, that the method of address which he then made use of, was with an intent to win me to his lure the sooner, as he found I was ingenuous, and consequently unsuspecting; and that he knew women of sense, spirit, and good-nature, were sooner to be deceived under the mask of open friendship, than by any other artifice.—Is not this, now, the *very magnanimity of manhood?*

While

While I was thus pleasing myself with my golden dream, word was sent us into the country, that my father had failed, that there was an execution in the house, that he himself was carried to jail, and that we had not a bed left to lie on.

I cannot describe what I felt on the news.—My mother went immediately to London, leaving me with our relation confined to my bed delirious, occasioned by this sudden change of circumstances: however, by the advantage of youth, and an excellent constitution, I recovered in about a week; and must confess, to my shame, that the distresses which my parents must suffer, were not so grievous to me as the reflection of what I must suffer, in not being able to shew my face among those of my acquainquaintance again, of whom I used to take the lead in all parties.

I was inconsolable; especially when I perceived an alteration in the behaviour of every person in the house where I then was.

Before they knew the misfortunes of my family, I was treated like a Queen, my look was a law, and every one seemed, by their eager watching what I wanted, to anticipate even my wishes by their ready attendance: but now the faces, the behaviour of every one was altered; they passed by me without curtseying: if I asked any of them to walk out, they were engaged; their heads ached; they were afraid it would rain; they did not chuse to go; and began to contradict me in every thing I proposed.

In about a week after I had left my room, juſt as we had ſat down to dinner, I was mentioning ſome fine partridges that I ſaw, when my relation, with all that matronly conſequence which prudiſh gravity can put on, told me it was not proper for me *now* to think of ſuch high living; that I ſhould ſuit my ideas to my circumſtances, and think, as I had nothing *now* left, that it was time for me to look out for ſomething; and that truly I ought to ſee for ſome ſervice, which would be better for me, than to remain a continual incumbrance on my friends.

I THREW down my knife and fork, and riſing almoſt choaked from table, went out of the houſe into a long elm walk at the back-gate, and there walking

ing backwards and forwards, ſtrove to give vent to my uneaſineſs.

LET whatever would be the conſequence, I was reſolved never to go into *that* houſe again.--" Service!--Service! "—Yes, (I ſaid, as I talked to myſelf) "—perhaps I may—perhaps I may " find ſome people, though ! at my ſer- " vice."—Then my fancy again was in an uproar; I ran over the catalogue of my admirers, and was certain I could not want friends.—I was determined.

THROUGH all my hiſtory the reader will find, that violent paſſions urged me into every inconvenience I experienced. —Let the more common-place ſcribblers, who borrow from the frippery of ſtale ſentiment thoſe Memoirs which they retail to the public; let them in

VOL. I.   H   their

their perfonages blame the villainies of the world, and the deceits, and the cruelties, and the many *et ceteras* which have made the characters they would celebrate unhappy. I was miferable merely by mifconduct. Vanity and felf-gratification firft ruined me; and by finding out the power of thofe two epidemics in others, I have fince made my fortune.

WHAT is called a proper fpirit of refentment brought me into numberlefs misfortunes; and though we may flatter ourfelves that revenge is noble, and that it is bafe not to refent injuries; I who know, if poffible, too much of both fexes, know that what we call demanding fatisfaction, arifes from the prejudice of falfe pride; and that we

ima-

imagine ourfelves entitled to more refpect than we receive. But if we would fhew ourfelves to be truly GREAT, the way to true greatnefs is as difficult to be found as the way to true gracefulnefs.

I WISH that both fexes would remember this plain piece of advice, but remember it practically: That

" THEY who refent injuries only equal
" their adverfaries; while they who for-
" give them always become fuperior."

WHILE I was walking in the Grove backwards and forwards, ruminating on my forlorn condition, a fhepherd's boy came to me, and in his aukward manner told me, that a very fine man wanted to fpeak to me at faather's.

I DID

I DID not underſtand the lad; but after bringing me, by taking hold of my gown, to the end of the walk, and pointing over the ſtile to a cottage, in the door-way of which I ſaw a very well-dreſs'd man ſtanding, the boy cried, " Yon yon felle, all with fine golden " cloaths on, wants you, madam, an' " pleaſe you."

I SENT the lad back, and bid him tell the perſon I did not underſtand any ſuch meſſage, and that I would not go. " Then," ſays the ruſtic, " I'll up- " hold, madam, that he'll gang tull " yow."

BEFORE I had taken three turns more the boy returned, and with him the perſon whom I had ſeen at a diſtance. When he came near enough for me to

ſee

see his face, I knew him to have been an intimate friend of my father's for some years, and one who always had expressed a particular esteem for me.

I CANNOT describe the surprize, nor the effect of that surprize, which I felt; but soon recovering, I considered, that perhaps, like my guardian angel, he was come to deliver me from my distress. I fancied his face told me so; and prospects of grandeur and pleasure began once more to fill my mind. But, fearful to discover myself by my looks, with downcast eyes I begged to know what part of my behaviour had ever given him encouragement to treat me in so abrupt a manner as to send for me: and by this time having recovered spirits enough, looking him full in the face, I asked him, if he thought that

that my father's misfortunes had broken *my* mind; or that, becaufe I could not command, as I ufed to do, I would be at any one's fervice who fent for me?

BENDING one knee to the ground, he begged my pardon; vowed he would do any thing he could for my happinefs: and began to ftammer, like a fchoolboy who is detected in a fib.—He hoped I would excufe him;--faid that he had fome reafons, which I fhould know hereafter, that prevented him from calling on me at my relation's houfe; that he came down on purpofe, after he had heard where I was, and was acquainted with the affairs of my family, to make me an offer of any part of his fortune I chofe to accept; and concluded with conjuring me to believe, that the propofal

pofal proceeded merely from difinterestedness.

Then it was that, for some moments, I experienced the so-seldom-to-be-felt pleasure, the love which has gratitude and esteem for its parents. But in this I did not long indulge myself; although from what he proffered, and the abjectness of my state, a thousand things, all in his favour, rose in my mind. My heart was at once his; and could he have forbore, but for some minutes, speaking over and over again concerning his disinterestedness, I should have confessed my affection, and gloried in the acknowledgement; for as yet I did not know his sex. But he cooled my first ardour by his own folly; for he endeavoured so much to make me believe that his offers to me originated

purely

purely from difintereftednefs, that I could not help fufpecting them.

But it is generally fo with Men, efpecially in their connections with our fex: they deceive themfelves, while they think they cheat us; and are weak enough to be impofed on by their own vanity, when they imagine they are making fools of us.

I do not deny but that many an unwary, inexperienced young woman, by the temptation of fine cloaths, fine words, a treat or two, and a few tawdry prefents, is led aftray and ruined (as 'tis called); and yet even thefe have moft commonly, before that time, notwithftanding all the many melancholy ftories told about forlorn run-away maidens by captains and rakes, &c. I fay, many even

of

of thefe damfels have, before their beau acquaintance, difpofed of their firft favours to their fathers plough-boys.

However, having acquainted him with the ill ufage which I had received from the people at whofe houfe I had been, and of my determination never to fet foot in it again, I confented to let him fend a poft-chaife from Tadcafter for me. We parted with, as I fuppofed, equal happy hopes; I to be reinftated in former fplendor; and he, as I imagined, pleafed with the profpect of my being his, without the fatigue of matrimony.

If any nice, delicate-minded reader fhould defpife me for being fo ready to yield my perfon merely to gratify my luxury; before they blame me, or any of my fex for thefe condefcenfions, let them

them look upon mankind, examine how they came by their grandeur, and I ſhall not be deemed to hazard too much in aſſerting, that the males will be found to be the worſt proſtitutes.

I WENT to the ſhepherd's cottage, and ſent for my cloaths; ſoon after which the chaiſe came to the door; when without even the common ceremony of a farewell to my former acquaintance (for I could not bear to ſpeak to any of the family) I ſet forward. As ſoon as the boy whipped his horſe on, my heart bounded with joy. I was now freed from the ill looks, dependence, and the reproaches of the ſordid wretches I had been with. I felt a ſudden ſatiſfaction at my alteration of place at leaſt.

I KNEW my deliverer, as I called him, had a great eſtate—I therefore indulg'd
myſelf

myself in several golden dreams —— and in some thoughts which I must own were not the most innocent; because I resolved not, nay I scorned, to be ungrateful: and as this gentleman had set out upon so disinterested a plan, I determined to be as generous, and not even wear a look of reproach or resentment, nor be ungratefully coy. Gratitude and desire took up all my thoughts; and I felt such an agitation of mind, that I was afraid I should hardly forbear throwing my arms about his neck, as he stood to receive me when I should alight from the post-chaise.

But extreme delicacy saved me; and, what is very surprising, extreme delicacy on the man's side; for when I came to Tadcaster, from whence he had sent the chaise, I found a note left for me, the

the purport of which was, "That to treat a person of my breeding with that delicacy I deserved, the people where I had lived should not say, I went from their house with any gentleman; and therefore hoped I would forgive him, if he waited for me at Doncaster; where he should bespeak a supper, which he hoped I should honour with my company. His elaborate epistle concluded with several protestations of love, sincerity, esteem, delicacy, and disinterestedness.

ALTHOUGH it was upon a mistaken principle, yet as I had reconciled myself to the granting this gentleman the last favour, I fed my vanity in considering the raptures he would be in, the homage he would pay me, and what an impression my alteration of dress would have

on

on him; for after we parted, I had taken fome pains with myfelf: yet, as I looked in the glafs, a figh efcaped me, and for a moment I confidered myfelf only as a dreffed victim.—But when I reflected that it was the facrifice of virtue to generofity, inclination, expectation, at the fame time taking part with my defign, I even applauded my conduct. I muft confefs, to be difappointed—honeftly I dare own it, I was monftroufly chagrined.

AFTER I had read the abovementioned letter, I bit my lips, and fuppofe I looked filly enough.—I could not but own his behaviour was polite, and all that; yet juft then—I don't know—- But why fhould I *now* be afhamed of what I *then* thought? Though I have made my fortune by affectation, I def-

pife

pife it; to be plain, therefore, with the reader, as I was determined to have made a noble prefent to him of my perfon, I was horridly piqued to be difappointed: it argued at leaft, as I fancied, a great want of fpirit in my admirer.

TRAVELLING to the next ftage gave me ftill further time to reflect on (as I thought) his very fingular behaviour. I began to think very indifferently of his intellects. My fpirits fubfided into a ftate of infipidity, and I ftepped out of the poft-chaife at Doncafter as cool as a ftage-coach paffenger; and gave him my hand with as little emotion, as if we had been married twenty years.

WE fupped together: but it was not in my conftitution at that time to be
long

long difpaffionate. The company of the landlady, who fat at table with us; the common chit-chat during fupper; the applaufe I received for almoft every word I fpoke, hurried me once more into fpirits, and I began again to be all-glowing with generofity, or, if you pleafe, with defire. Our hoftefs being juft then called out, my deliverer took that opportunity to falute me. His kifs (for he dwelt upon my lips) flew thro' my veins like fubtle poifon.—I was alarmed at my conftitution.—I begged he would defift; but in fuch a tone— he was no judge; for, obedient as a flave, he bowed, refumed his feat, begged my pardon, and again mentioned difintereftednefs.

I BLUSHED; but it was with vexation. I thought it a depravity in his tafte,

that

that he could be so very tame.—I could not answer him; I looked down; and pride reproached me for my eagerness to surrender to a man who did not deserve such a prize. Self-reproach made me for some time hate myself, that I could more earnestly wish to be ruined, than my lover was assiduous to accomplish it.

He took hold of my hand, and raised it to his lips: I felt my fever returning. I begged he would not offer to take hold of me: "Since (as I told him) he had declared himself my disinterested friend, I begged he would be what he pretended, and leave the reward to be determined by his deserts; and that he might be sure of my gratitude."

How

How much are our sex sometimes beholden to the diffidence, irresolution, or want of understanding, among mankind!

He immediately let go my hand, and vowed most solemnly henceforth to treat me as if I was his Sister.

I could have spit in his face for such an answer.

" Believe me, madam, (he added)
" my actions shall always to you be ad-
" dressed with the most becoming de-
" licacy."

It was with difficulty I could restrain myself from laughing in his face

" I have long adored my angel."

I thought

I THOUGHT him a very silly fellow.

HE then begged to know my opinion of him.

I WAS silent--but could not help hating him.

ONCE more he told me his fortune was at my service; and poured a purse full of guineas into my lap.

AT that moment I could not think him entirely shocking.

" WHAT muſt I do with this?" I aſked him.

" PUT it up, I beg of you, madam.
" —Stay, I am ſorry to give you that
" trouble; let me put them into the
" purſe again." He did ſo; and then,
after

after many intreaties, I put the money into my pocket.

AFTER this, he begged once more to falute me.

BUT I, looking graver than before, defired to know, if he imagined the prefent he had juft made me had prevailed with me? or, did he think I was to be bought?

" No, madam, the world's wealth
" cannot purchafe you:—I once more
" beg pardon, I am anfwered."

VERY eafily, I thought.

THE landlady's return prevented our further parley. The converfation became more general; but in fpite of my
gal-

gallant's difinterestedness, I could perceive that he was, by all the schemes he could practise, endeavouring to make me drink a glass of wine; nay, he once or twice endeavoured to trick me into drinking a bumper; and appealed to our hostess; who, good, kind, condescending soul! answered with an—" O,
" yes, Sir,——to be sure, Sir,——my
" lady, I dare say, won't refuse your
" Honour.——And indeed—but I beg
" pardon—yet our claret, as my Lady
" Duchess told me, is the best claret
" upon the road; and really, Mem, I
" hope no offence, but you have not
" drank a glass *sense* supper."

NEITHER will I, thought I; for now I could see through his wretched plot, and despised him heartily.

He

He had not spirit, nor understanding, to win me with my senses about me, but rather chose to be indebted to senseless intoxication for enjoyment, than generous inclination. O Man, Man! I at this time wondered at his stupidity; but experience has since instructed me, that he was not a jot less dull than the major part of his brother-lovers.

I ORDERED the maid to shew me to bed And now do not you, ye prudes, pretend to dread reading any further, lest you should meet with any wanton descriptions that might alarm your sensibilities, and you should be *so* shocked at such obscene writing, that you could not be able to think—of any thing else.

Fr.

For to fatisfy, or, to fpeak more honeftly, to diffatisfy you, in this work there fhall not be any of thofe commonplace pictures or defcriptions which only tend to make weak minds ftill weaker; this work being intended as a Dissection of the Mind; to lay nature naked to view; but not in that manner which is at prefent practifed by fome Life-writers, who imagine a lufcious page is a proof of a writer's genius.—Want of decency, however, is want of fenfe; and this has been my remark through the almoft incredible fcenes of riot which I have been engaged in, That every man and woman deviated from decency in proportion to their deficiency of underftanding.

In the morning, reflecting on my own fituation, on the condition to which my

parents

parents were reduced, and on the extreme backwardnefs of my lover, I refolved to come to an explanation at once with him; and determined, if he would be the means of reinftating my father, to yield myfelf entirely to his will. At the fame time refolving to let him know my determination immediately, I rung the bell, informed the chambermaid I would breakfaft in bed, and told her to let the gentleman, who fupped with me laft night, know, that I fhould be glad of his company to drink a difh of tea with me.

AFTER the tea-things were carried down, without much apology I confeffed my defign to him, and he gave me his promife.---Don't laugh at me, reader, or think that, young as I then was, and unhackneyed in the ways of life, I

could

could be such an idiot to rely on a man's promise—No; I had his promissory note for 500 l. before I would admit him to the least liberty.

We immediately came to London, and he hired me very genteel apartments near St. James's. The next day after my arrival in Town, I paid a visit to my disconsolate father in the Fleet, and made him an offer of all the money I had about me, which amounted to upwards of fifty guineas ; but neither would he nor my mother receive a shilling of it, until they knew how I came by it.

My blood was chilled at their refusal; I looked upon them with astonishment. I fell down on my knees, and confessed what I had committed ; but to

pal-

palliate my offence, told them, it was done with an intention of having my father enlarged, and fet up again in the world; and fhewed them the note for 500 l. which I offered to them.

BOTH however refufed it; and at the fame time refufed any longer to acknowledge me for their daughter. I fell at their feet. They turned me out of their miferable lodging-room; and forbade me ever to fee them again, unlefs I returned all my ill-acquired wealth.

O HOW did their words pierce me, when they faid, " That they could " bear want and imprifonment, but " they would never partake of the wa- " ges of proftitution."

I WENT home determined to break off my criminal connection; to renounce dress, equipage, and every other sinful accumulation, by way of expiation for what I had committed; to live with my parents as their servant; and to endure all the inclemencies such a state of servitude, in such a place, could bring on me.

But when I arrived there, and looking round my apartments, saw every thing in such elegance—such furniture, and all my own too!—good heavens! was it possible, young, unexperienced, and vain as I was, I could persuade myself to quit them?—And then, as I stood by the glass, tho' my eyes were red with crying, yet I could not help thinking it a pity, that such a figure as I was should do the drudgery of a scullion in a prison; and instead of the dress I then wore, to change it for a ragged gown, a dirty apron, and every other mark with which extreme poverty cloaths its labourers.—

I was

I was shocked at the thought; I could not bear it—No—I considered, I could do my family more good, though unknown to them, by getting money, than by being their servant.

- I DETERMINED to lay by one-half of all I was or should be worth, towards reinstating them; and resolved on a scheme by which it might be done, and they not know that any pecuniary assistance came from my wages of prostitution. Thus I began to fortify myself in my conduct. I imagined I was behaving praise-worthily, and thought I could not be accounted criminal, since it was to serve my father and mother.

IN like manner are we all self-fooled; we gloss over our guilt with virtue's varnish—all find excuses for their vices and follies.

The man who, at a nation's expence, heaps up immenfe riches, and accumulates unwieldy eftates, by fetting the intereft of his country to fale;—that very man reconciles thefe tranfactions to himfelf, by faying, " I do thefe things " for the good of my family."

He who betrays the fecrets of his friend to his patron, for which he gets fome worthlefs finecure, makes fuch behaviour eafy to his own mind, by telling himfelf, that " fuch things fhould " not be hid."

Does not the Man of Pluralities tell us, that we are not to throw away the good things of this world? and that he or fhe only are fools, who might ride in their own coaches, and will not do it; but rather trudge honeft and dirty
through

through the streets, splashed and thrust aside by every saucy footman, or more insolent chairman, who perhaps is bearing successful villainy to pay a visit to ※※※?

YET, even in this life, I know it, and so do we all, that *there is a time* when Nature, or the alarm of Nature, *Remorse*, will be heard; when the multitude of wax-lights cannot dispel the inward gloom; when myriads of attendants cannot drive away that guest, nor the brilliant stomacher be a shield of proof against it.

AT that time I was shocked with the thought of becoming a scullion; of leaving all the gaieties of life to become a poor drudge: but had I then known what I afterwards experienced, I should have been convinced, that the poor drudge

drudge does not labour half so much as a Prostitute; that she—the Prostitute I mean—is beneath the basest scullion; subject to every man's depravities; ever in alarms; in her best station but like a gilded coffin, an outside glare, filled with corruption; and in a state of poverty, the most abject and most despicable of all beings.

I was maintained in the utmost splendor by my Keeper, his vanity making him *shew me off* (as he called it) in all the extravagance of the mode. I was followed at every public place, addressed by love-letters, songs were made upon me, and metzotinto pictures of me sold at all the print-shops: in short, I grew into such fame, that I was the general toast among men of fortune, while the

ladies.

ladies borrowed their fashions from what
I wore.

But my friend, like several others of his sex, was dissatisfied with what he enjoyed, unless he could tell the whole world how happy he was; he had therefore every week private parties to sup with him at my apartments. There I was obliged to suffer him to treat me with all that fondling familiarity, that childish toying, with which some new-married people expose themselves before company—every minute kissing, or lolling upon one another's necks, patting cheeks, playing with lips, or talking like babies.

I was at first ashamed of behaving so; but he soon made me so frequently repeat it, that this *precious foolery* became quite

quite indifferent to me, then fatiguing, and at laſt loathſome.

I DARED not refuſe him, though ſuch fulſome behaviour made me ſick—I was obliged to practiſe it.—What could I do? I could not bear the thoughts of living leſs elegant.—*There was the rub.*——— Pride, curſed pride, the affectation to appear fine, is the ruin of both ſexes. To indulge ourſelves in unwarrantable luxuries; to gratify that mean, falſe paſſion, we women ſubmit to ſlaveries incredible; and, like the worthleſs time-ſerving flatterer, we ſacrifice our minds to the bribery of proſtitution.

I DREADED every appointment which this man made. I knew what a night I had to go through. I have felt my heart ſink, when he has begun with,
 " Betſy,

"Betſy, I ſhall have company to-night "at your houſe." No truant ſchoolboy could be more dejected after conviction. I reflected that, ſpaniel-like, I muſt play over all the common tricks before company, of fondling and fooling.

Is it any wonder, then, that Kept-Miſtreſſes generally deſpiſe their Keepers, and like every man better than he who maintains them? It is becauſe our Keepers behave worſe to us than any other men do. They have bought us, and every Engliſh woman, I am certain, though ſhe ſubmits to be ſold, deſpiſes the chapman. Money indeed ſhe has no objection to, and therefore loves the treaſon, though ſhe hates the traitor.

When

WHEN we are in company with the man of our choice, we can give a loofe to fancy, and unreftrained indulge every wifh, in the inftant of inclination. We ftart fair for pleafure,—and leave hypocrify far behind :—No bartering there, but each generoufly and unaffectedly giving a loofe to defire, we appear ALL OURSELVES.

BUT on him who pays us our penfions we are obliged to wait; to watch his languid appetite; to take pains to heighten his paffion by fulfome fondnefs and feigned tranfports; not a thought, not a wifh of our own confulted.—Yet we *muft* do it.---He pays us; and when a man purchafes our perfons, he imagines that our minds muft be toffed into the bargain; and that we are obliged, at a moment's warning, to call up all the

vigour

vigour of affection for him, and even aid his appetite; which renders our state more fatiguing, more diftafteful.

YET though I bore thefe difgraces with difguft, I had not commenced any new intrigue. I had indeed received feveral letters from many who fubfcribed themfelves my admirers, and who talked of their eftates, their honours, and their fettlements. Fear, however, kept me fometimes undetermined; fometimes the folly of my own man's behaviour made me fick of the whole fex; and fometimes the manner in which feveral of thefe letters were wrote, made me defpife the writers.

WERE I to publifh a collection of the genuine fond epiftles which I have by me, written too by perfons who call themfelves themselves *fine gentlemen*, my readers would wonder there could be any man of fortune and figure so illiterate; yet I have epistles to prove that there are many men who value themselves—arrogantly value themselves—upon their birth and breeding, who can neither spell true, nor write proper English; and whose stile is as uncouth as the shape of their letters.

ALL the company which I kept of my own sex were ladies of the same profession, and in high keeping; and, as the phrase is, *were happy women.*— But how strangely do we confound together two such contradictory terms as *happiness* and *prostitution!*

EVERY one of these ladies had, as I found, a gentleman or two whom they used ufed to meet privately, and from whom they ufed to receive very handfome prefents. This I thought at firft dangerous, and told them fo. They ftared at me when I informed them that I never had wronged my friend, either out of inclination or intereft, and eafily perfuaded me to become one of their party.

THE next morning, when my lover, or *friend*, (which is the more fafhionable word) had left me, I was told a lady defired to fpeak to me.

ON her entering the room, I never was fo much prejudiced in favour of any perfon, at firft fight, before. She feemed to be a woman of about fifty, tall, ftraight and genteel; her complexion was clear, and her eyes gliftened with fenfibility. In her addrefs I thought

thought too I could perceive the woman of diſtinction; for her deportment bore an eaſe and dignity that was truly amiable.

After ſome previous compliments and apologies, ſhe informed me, that having been very genteely brought up, but moſt unfortunately married, neceſſity had forced her to comply ſo far with the depravity of the times, as to keep a private Aſſembly-room; where the politeſt gentlemen in England, and they only, were admitted; and where a ſelect party of ladies met to play at cards, dance country-dances, or kill an hour in any other agreeable amuſements.

I was not a little aſtoniſhed, when I found that this lady was neither more nor leſs than a downright Procureſs; yet there

there was something in her manner so entertaining, that I begged she would let me know how I could be any ways serviceable to her, as I had already conceived a friendship for her.

The ideas which I had entertained of those *charitable matrons* who take pains to bring both sexes together, and whose common and vulgar title is *Bawd*, in nothing resembled this lady, either in person or behaviour. They are in general unwieldy, swinish figures; as vulgar in their conversation, as depraved in their principles; base, low, villanous-bred; and, like pimps, the very outcasts of the creation.

But this lady was equally genteel in her person, address, and conversation. She informed me, that the ladies who visited her,

her, were selected for the delicacy of their figures as well as of their manners; and after complimenting me that I should grace her Assembly, begged I would dine that day with her, and be myself a judge from appearances of what I might expect :---" For believe me, madam,
" (thus she went on) I have seen so
" much of the world, as to smile when
" I hear persons talk about virtue,
" conscience, self-denial, and such stuff.
" I grant you, indeed, there are such
" things in the world, and that some
" people possess them; but they are
" a very trifling minority. The Mil-
" lion love indulgencies; and if a
" man of fortune will pay for pleasure,
" it is proper that he should be gratifi-
" ed. None but men of the first fashion
" visit me, madam, at my Assembly;
and

" and you will likewife find no impofi-
" tions at my houfe; no forcing liquor
" down; nor are you obliged to pay fo
" much per cent. which is called *Pound-*
" *age*, to any-body, out of what you
" are prefented with. You are now,
" madam, in your bloom; ufe it as peo-
" ple do their intereft at elections,
" make the beft market you can for
" yourfelf; for, believe me, in fpite of
" the cant about integrity, and honour,
" and generofity, and fuch terms, all
" the good qualities upon earth, when
" you grow old, if you have not
" money to back them, will hardly
" make intereft enough for you to get
" into a workhoufe."

I DINED with her that day in St. James's Place. At dinner there was an elegant fideboard of plate. She had also a servant waiting in livery; and after the cloth was taken away, as there was no other company, she thus opened herself to me.

" You see, my dear, the manner in
" which my house is furnished, and the
" neighbourhood in which I live : no
" clamours, no ill treatment can be ex-
" perienced here. You seem to have
" a mind susceptible of most powerful
" sensations; I beg therefore you will
" allow me to give you one word of
" advice.—Above all things, avoid be-
" ing fond of any man. For a lady of
" pleasure to be in love, is the worst
" distemper she can be seized with.
" Never, therefore, if you can help it,
" keep clever fellows company. You
" will find very few of them among
monied

" monied men; therefore suffer the
" rich only to visit you; you will be
" heart-whole with them, I assure you.
" But never have any thing (if you
" can help it) to say to a man of wit
" or humour.

" I confess, there is a female tri-
" umph which our minds indulge in,
" when we are admired by such people.
" But what good can such persons do a
" lady?----Will genius pay for a dia-
" mond necklace? or wit and invention
" make her a settlement? Yes, if she
" could live upon the air, they would
" allow her all the fee-simple of Parnas-
" sus, and she might chuse what part
" of the clouds she pleased for her se-
" curity.

Yet

" YET I, like the reft of the world,
" give advice I cannot follow.---I have
" ruined myfelf with them, nay yet
" doat upon them; for, in fpite of all
" our refolutions, in the hour of inclina-
" tion who can withftand them?

" HOWEVER, madam, I'll tell you of
" fome gentlemen who ufe my houfe,
" and to whom, if you pleafe, and
" when you pleafe, I will introduce
" you. They are not men of wit and
" humour, but they are HUMOURISTS,
" who love to be indulged in fome fin-
" gularities, which ladies who have fenfe
" enough to fuffer, find their account
" in it, by the handfome prefents that
" are made to them.

" You may fit with any of them a
" whole night, and not find them guil-
" ty

" ty of saying a good thing, nor of
" doing one, except parting with their
" money, which they do as freely as
" I give my servants small-beer.

" This is their night of meeting;
" they have a club here once a week.
" You shall go with me into my little
" sweet-meat closet, from whence we
" can have a full view of them as
" they come in; and I'll give you
" their separate histories."

Mrs. Ealsy then conducted me to the closet abovementioned, where she gave me a description of her guests, as they passed by; and which she did so much to their discredit, that I began to despise mankind most heartily.

THE

THE gay FLORIO was the firſt who came in. He, it ſeems, had married a young lady, of a very good family, only ſix months before.—Though this was a match of love, yet in three weeks after wedlock he grew tired of his wife, came to this houſe, and here divert himſelf with having a ſet of creatures about him ſelected from the loweſt dregs of the people: the more abandoned, the more vulgar the women, the more agreeable were they to his taſte.

OLD C— was the next we ſaw, with both feet wrapped about with flannel; and who by the help of two crutched-ſticks, hobbled from his chair in purſuit of proſtitute Beauty.

As

As foon as Mrs. EALSY faw him fhe turned to me, and faid, " My dear, " this gentleman I will introduce you " to; you'll find it vaftly worth your " while ;" and immediately ringing the bell, ordered a fervant to wait upon his Honour with her compliments, and " to let his Honour know, that " fhe would attend upon his Honour " prefently, with *fomething,* fhe hoped, " very much to his Honour's fatisfac-
" tion."

SHE would not, however, ufher me to this gouty gallant until fhe had told me his hiftory; which was as follows.

" His father had been bred up, from " an errand-boy, tapfter at one of the " largeft inns at York, and there he " married one of the chambermaids.
" They

" They fet up a pot-houfe; and in a
" little time after, fhe was delivered
" of the very perfon we faw juft now,
" who was fo richly dreffed, and fo in-
" firm, and who being taken by a York-
" fhire 'fquire to be a ftable-helper, and
" runner of errands, came up to Lon-
" don with his mafter as a poftilion.

" HAVING had a common country-
" fchool education, he was, by means
" of his mafter's fifter, for whom he had
" managed feveral intrigues, recom-
" mended by her, on her marriage
" with Lord —, to be an Under-clerk
" in one of the Public Offices.

" THERE, by his bearing every
" thing from his fuperiors, telling
" every thing to them, never refufing
" any thing they afked him to do, and
" con-

" convincing them that he had no re-
" gard to any one moral, social, or
" grateful tie, contradictory to what
" they should approve; he was soon
" raised to a station which brought
" him 300l. *per annum.*

" He boarded all this time along
" with a widow, whose only daughter,
" by his hypocritical behaviour, and
" from her not having been ever used
" to converse with the world, he had
" brought to look upon him with af-
" fection. Her figure was amazingly
" beautiful; she was about seventeen
" years of age, and the amiableness of
" her temper was even superior to the
" loveliness of her person.

" He intended marrying the daugh-
" ter, although his spirit was too da-
" hardly

" hardly to think of any fatisfaction
" which might arife from the poffef-
" fion of fuch a treafure. He only
" confidered, from the number of
" examples which he by this time had
" had opportunities of being an eye
" or ear witnefs to, that a handfome
" wife is the fureft recommendation
" for a hufband to make his fortune
" by.

" ONE evening, however, after the
" mother's as well as her daughter's con-
" fent had been obtained, the wedding
" was fixed for the following week;
" when, as he was walking with her in
" Vauxhall-Gardens, my L— B— met
" them; who feeing fo lovely a crea-
" ture, was immediately ftruck with
" her, and knowing her hufband that
" was

" was to be, joined company with
" them.

" This nobleman, who never knew
" what it was to check any of his wifhes
" that expence and ftratagem could
" gratify, and who was confcious of the
" paffive obedience and venality of his
" man, immediately looked upon this
" young creature as his own: and in
" a very fhort time indeed fhe became
" fo. She was married, it is true, to
" this very man, who entered juft now,
" but who put his Lordfhip to bed to
" her in his own ftead, and for which
" he obtained a lucrative poft in Ja-
" maica, whither he went the week
" following. In a few years he accu-
" mulated a large fum of money, and
" hearing from England that his firft
" wife was dead, he married a rich

" Cre-

" Creole's daughter, the greatest beauty
" in that country.

" WITH her and her fortune he ar-
" rived safe in England, just before the
" war, and appeared with his lady in
" all public places. So showy a figure
" could not fail of presently attracting
" admirers; and as he then began to
" affect hospitality, his table seldom
" wanted guests: for such is the pre-
" sent noble-spirited disposition of the
" times, that every man is sure of a
" prodigious number of friends, pro-
" vided he has but any thing which
" they may think worth their stealing
" from him. For example,

" THE young gentleman of much
" ready-money, as soon as his taste is
" known to be for play, is continually
" fur-

" furrounded by gamblers; who, with
" all the feeming affiduities of fervice,
" are every day picking his pocket.

" Any man of great intereft has his
" table furrounded with a fet of hun-
" gry Parafites, Informers, Pimps, and
" proud beggars, who wait open-
" mouthed, like children at bob-cher-
" ry, in hopes each to fnatch depen-
" dent preferment.

" If a gentleman has a handfome
" wife, has he not immediately an infi-
" nite number of friends ftart up, like
" fo many Dæmons by the power of
" incantation, ready to do him any
" fervice?

" This was the cafe with the perfon
" whofe ftory I am relating:—but he
" had

"had meanness enough to suffer his
"wife to commit any actions she pleas-
"ed, provided they tended to one
"point—the point of self-interest.

"Whether it was or was not con-
"certed between them, I cannot be
"positive; but he surprised a very
"Great Man, one afternoon, in a very
"familiar conversation with his wife.
"Instead of alarming the neighbour-
"hood, or bringing his cause into
"Westminster-Hall, he compromised
"the affair, forgave his spouse upon
"her submission, and accepted of a
"Commissary's post, as a retaliation
"for the injury he received from
"the Great Man; set out for the
"Continent in a few days, as the
"war was upon the point of breaking
"out; returned upon the signing of the
"pre-

" preliminary articles; and now lives
" happy with his lady, and enjoys a
" fortune (all of his own getting!)
" of above 20,000l. *per annum*.

" 'Tis true, he loves to recreate
" himself now and then here, and his
" wife don't grumble, becaufe he al-
" lows her the fame liberty. He is
" likewife a moft generous creature
" to any lady he likes; and therefore
" I will introduce you to him."

UPON this Mrs. EALSY, taking me
by the hand, led me down to his Honour.

THE perfon to whom Mrs. EALSY introduced me, expreffed himfelf to be
uncommonly pleafed with my company;
thought no expence too much for me;
made

made me refuse all other male visitors; and became so intolerably fond of me, that I was almost distracted.

I HATED him, however, because he was fulsome; I despised him for the indelicacy of his manners, or, as he called it, of his taste; and his jealousy was almost insupportable.

I LIVED in luxury, 'tis true, but did not enjoy one hour's satisfaction. My affections were unfixed; I had strong desires, which were not satisfied, as I had no object I could indulge them with; and as to my Keeper!—But, indeed, all Keepers are to *us* the same; we never can relish the man who gives us money: we love the treason, but hate the traitor.

SUCH

Such are the fentiments of every one of our profeffion who is a real Woman of the Town. We have more pleafure in one hour in the company of the man whom we treat, than in a feven years fociety with the man who maintains us. We are forced to be fond of thofe who pay us for it; their careffes, therefore, are fo many torments, and every one of their kiffes is teizing.

Never was man more liberal to his Miftrefs than my elderly lover was to me; yet never did woman do lefs to deferve his bounty than I did. But my indifference, perhaps, kept his affection alive; for men are odd creatures even in their appetites.

His jealoufy, however, diftracted me. I was obliged to be continually at home, as his coming was uncertain; and was therefore no more than a fine-dreffed prifoner. Unlefs I went out with him or to meet him, I had not the liberty to ftir except to the mercer's, and then an old fervant he had, ufed to attend me there and back again.

I SIGHED for freedom; I wanted to be lefs glaring and more happy. I envied every woman, even in a check'd apron. Comparing my coop'd-up condition with her's, I confidered myfelf to be no more than a flave; like mifers' gold, locked up from every body but one man to feaft himfelf with.

'Tis true, my wifhes were prevented by the profufenefs of his prefents: yet thofe prefents could never tempt me to make him any affectionate, any grateful return;

return; becaufe I ufed to recollect how dearly I earned every fum of money I received, every trinket he gave me.

At laft, however, the time was at hand, when I was to repent of my behaviour. For it happened, that going to the mercer's to look at fome Spring patterns, as I ftepp'd out of my chariot my foot flipped, and in fpite of my footman's immediate affiftance I muft have fallen, had not a gentleman, at that inftant paffing by, caught me in his arms, and carried me into the fhop.

After I had fat down, he addreffed me very agreeably on my efcape, made fome whimfical remarks upon the accident, and congratulated himfelf on the lucky part he bore in my deliverance with fo much

much humour and spirit, that his conversation charmed me.

I DWELT more and more on every syllable he said.—Unperceived by him, I now and then looked at his figure.— It was amiable,—his look sensible, and his address delicately tender. I loved him, really loved; he was, in short, the first man who ever possessed my inclinations. Many, indeed, had been made to believe I loved them; and they believed it, because they used to ask me to tell them so.

" Do you love me, my dear girl?"— What a question is that! Thus some guests, when they enter a tavern, will ask the master if he has any good wine in the house? What answer can such persons expect, either from lady or vintner,

vintner, but—" To be sure, Sir, you
" need not doubt it,—upon my ho-
" nour, Sir."

I STAID at the mercer's as long as I
conveniently could; and in the course
of conversation, I found my favourite
was but that day arrived in London;
that he only came to town from mo-
tives of curiosity; and that he put up
in Holborn, at the York-stage inn.

ALL that night, with my Keeper by my
side, I lay awake thinking on this young
fellow:—it was impossible for me to
sleep; for, as it is said in the play,
" He had murdered sleep." I appeal
to any woman who has been in my situation, who has loved one man, and has
had another whom she detested lollop-
ing along-side of her, what a com-
fortable

fortable time she must have before breakfast.

A PENNY-POST letter told the stranger to expect me at his Inn in the afternoon; and in less than ten days from that visit we landed together at Calais, I having previously converted all my plate, furniture, &c. into cash, which in three years was all expended.—But then it was gloriously laid out : so much pleasure for so much money !—I pleased myself, and that is all which the greatest can pretend to.—I had long been a slave to others' pleasure, I now resolved to be free for my own.—It is true, I paid dear for the resolution—I ruined myself by it.—What then ? Throughout my whole life, I never once thought it worth my while to reflect on the consequences of what I intended to do; it was

was sufficient for me that I liked the scheme, and that determined me to pursue it.

THEY who only know the human heart by hearsay pretend to argue, that no Woman of the Town can be fond of any particular person, so unsatisfied are we in our desires. This, however, is a rank falsehood. We are indeed tolerable judges of mankind; and it is that knowledge which makes us so indifferent to the fondness and dalliance of the generality of men.

WE treat monied men complaisantly, in the same manner that other tradespeople do their ready-money customers. Every man is alike to us who pays us; figure, understanding, accomplishments, are all absorbed in that one article: but
in

in the man who hits our fancy, we neither confider figure, accomplifhments, nor underftanding. If he does but win our inclinations, let him be ugly, poor, and a fool, 'tis all the fame. Let him even behave as he pleafes, when once we are fixed, it pleafes us; fo wretched is the depravity of the tafte which muft attend upon Proftitution.

On returning with my favourite man from our tour, the laft guinea we had in the world was changed on the day we landed in England; and yet both of us were as full of fpirits, as if we had been going to take poffeffion of 10,000l. a year.—While Satisfaction ftays at home, it always faves the heart from aching. Thus it was with us; we poffeffed a great deal, we were rich in each other's arms:

arms: as to any thing elfe, it was not worth fighing for.

As we were at dinner, however, the next day, my lover fell down fpeechlefs, and expired inftantaneoufly. Then I became inconfolable. After his death, misfortunes hundred-fold ftared me in the face; I fell violently ill the next day, kept my room above a month, and on my recovery found that the woman who had been hired for my nurfe, had robbed me of every thing I poffeffed.

WITH much difficulty I arrived in London, without any other dependance but my perfon for my maintenance; and in my prefent miferable circumftances I could not fet that off in any faleable light.

In a moſt forlorn condition I took a back garret in one of the ſtreets near the Seven Dials.

Vice is not only callous to remorſe, but alſo to ſhame; for notwithſtanding the miſery to which I was reduced, I never really repented; that is, with true contrition. My ſighs were like thoſe of a ſtript gameſter; I was mad at my misfortunes, but never intended to leave off my former practices.

I grieved for my change of circumſtances, but it was a grief which proceeded from pride; not an affliction from the horrors of a miſ-ſpent life, but a chagrin occaſioned by my knowing that I was deprived of the means of making the ſame figure in Town as formerly.

I now

I now commenced common street-walker; but as if it was ordained that mifery fhould ftill be made more wretched, the firft evening I took my ftand in Fleet-ftreet, to look out for a fare, I was drove from ftreet to ftreet by women of my own profeffion, who fwore I fhould not come in their *beats* until I had paid my *footing*.

Not having a fingle farthing, I knew not what to do. One of them fnatched the only handkerchief I had in the world off my neck, while another pulled off my cap and kept it. I had been the whole day making thefe two pieces of finery up, out of the fragments of the laft gauze apron I had left; and after wafhing them and fmoothing them myfelf, in hopes by fuch baits to tempt fomebody to enable me to purchafe a meal's meal's meat for the next day, having not broke my faſt that day, I turned out. What then muſt be my deſpair, to find myſelf even deprived of the hope of being in a condition to earn ſix-pence, to preſerve myſelf from famiſhing!

At that inſtant a woman's voice called out from ſome diſtance, " Beſs, " Beſs, the Informers are coming!" My perſecutors fled from me immediately, and left me bare-headed and bare-necked. My hair was very long, of a very good colour, and the complexion both of my face and neck clear, and without any artifice to ſet it off: I could not, even if I had choſe it, have paid even for a pennyworth of Spaniſh red. In that figure I ſtood difconſolate, like Jane Shore (as I ſuppoſe
ſhe

she appeared) when she set out to do penance.

Before I had time to consider what I should do, I was seized by two men, who laid hold of me by the arms and shoulders, saying, " So, Madam, what
" you had a mind to be taken, it
" seems? What, you staid here to see
" what we were about, did you, hah?
" What, you wou'dn't sculk off when
" the rest did, though you knew we
" were coming, hah?—I suppose you
" had a mind to turn spy, but we'll
" take care"———

I replied, " Indeed, gentlemen"—

They would not, however, suffer me to go on; and one of them interrupting me very surlily, made answer,—
" Do

" Do you prate, you brazen-faced
" b——h ? Don't you know who we
" are, b—ft you ? that we belong to
" the Society for the Reformation of
" Manners, Mrs. *Bunter?* and will, for
" the glory of God, and the honour of
" Religion, carry you to Bridewell for
" whoring, huffy ?"

I now fell down on my knees, and begged them, for God's fake, to have pity upon me. I confeffed to them, that I came from home, indeed, with an intent to be a whore, to offer myfelf to any body who would give me any thing; but that I had not eat all that day; that this was my firft night of going out; that I was quite a ftranger; and that fome other women had pulled my handkerchief and cap off, and run
away

away with them for my *footing*, as they called it.

One of the men immediately faid to the other, " I fancy this is a green-" horn; let's take her to the lamp, " and look what fort of a face fhe has " got." On this they hauled me to a light; and one of them ftood ftaring in my face, while I, with difhevelled hair, naked neck, and the tears dropping down my cheeks, ftood in dreadful expectation of my fentence.

One of my fifters in fin, as I fuppofe, came by, and told the other Reformer fhe wanted to fpeak with him. As foon as he went with the woman, the other, who had been looking at me all that time, told me I fhould not go to Bridewell, but he would fee-me fafe to
my

my lodgings, and give me something to eat and drink.

I BELIEVE it is King Lear who says, " The act of our necessity is strange, " that can make vile things precious." I never went to any of my own elegant-furnished apartments with a tythe of that transport with which I now went back to my miserable garret; it was to me an elysium to be saved from Bridewell, and to be told that I should have something to eat and drink.

I PITY those of large possessions who never have been happy enough to be in distress; they can't enjoy—it is impossible—I dare insist on it, they can't enjoy half that satisfaction, nor half that true relish for any of life's conveniencies, which those have, who, after

feeling

feeling misery, have been reinstated in affluence.

I SUPPED with my new acquaintance; and grew in spirits. Next day he took me a better lodging, and after the neighbourhood were all at rest, he used to visit me.

I ENQUIRED why he was so cautious of coming to see me in the day-time; and what particular profits there could be in his office of Constable, that made it worth his while to be up so late almost every night.

UPON which, chucking me under the chin, he gave me the following history of himself.

HISTORY

OF A

REFORMING CONSTABLE.

"IF I was only a common Conſtable, my dear, it would be a poor ſervice, and no man would care to follow it; but I am one of the Reforming Conſtables: I belong to thoſe that ſerve the Church; I am one of Religion's officers, and Religion never lets any of her true ſervants want."

I ASKED him, how he could reconcile keeping me, and having a wife, to Religion?

"PHO, my dear, he replied, what I mean by the word Religion is, in

" my fignification, *Church-work.*—For
" mum!—but that's between ourfelves
" though—we are a parcel of d——'d
" fly fellows, and love to do a thing
" or two as well as another body, but
" don't care the world fhould know it.

" In the firft place now, every Wo-
" man that picks up between Charing-
" crofs and the Change, up Holborn,
" down Feet-lane, all the way to
" Tower-hill, *comes down to us* for
" every night's Liberty; and we ne-
" ver let them run above three nights
" in arrears: if they do, why we take
" them up for Proftitutes, for the ho-
" nour of our holy Religion.

" I was born at Nottingham. My
" father and mother being upon a
" march to join the regiment, my mo-
" ther'

"ther fell in labour there, and died in
"child-bed; fo the parifh-officers were
"obliged to take care of me, until
"they could let me out to thofe dealers
"who hire infants, and go about the
"country to beg with them.

"I was foon taken notice of to be
"a boy of parts; fo a tinker and chim-
"ney-fweeper played a rubber at Put
"who fhould take me 'prentice, and
"the tinker won.

"I then got acquainted with fome
"folks that ufed to go upon the Fo-
"reft and kill venifon. One day, how-
"ever, we were all taken up, and put
"into prifon, for being deer-ftealers;
"but as I was fo very young, nothing
"was done to me, and the gaoler made
"me tapfter-boy; and there fome gen-
"tlemen,

" tlemen, who were under fentence of
" tranfportation, taught me to read
" and write.

" THEN I hired myfelf to an inn, as
" as a helper to the book-keeper; but
" there being a little parcel loft with
" two guineas in it, and my mafter be-
" ing a fufpicious man, rather than
" have any words with him, I went
" away. Next I was a Waiter at Scar-
" borough; and I am fure, let the
" people fay what they will againft
" Gamefters, Gamblers, or Family-
" men, they were the beft cuftomers the
" houfe ever had.

" THEY ufed to come down every
" feafon, and I lived at the tavern
" which had the moft and beft com-
" pany ufed it; and thefe gentlemen
" of

" of the Family would leave with me
" so many new packs of stamped cards,
" and so many new stamped dice, so
" that I never had the trouble of going
" out to buy any. Then when any of
" the customers ordered me to go
" out to buy cards or dice, I would go
" to my room, and get them; at the
" same time I would swear I had been
" out, and bought them myself at the
" shops: however, I got well paid by
" the gentlemen I told you of before
" for my trouble and my swearing.

" At last I was taught how to be a
" Family-man myself; indeed, I learnt
" some of it with my tinker-master.
" So I came to London; but here I
" was taken up for a pick-pocket, be-
" cause I found a pocket-book at the
" play-house door.—I laid in gaol three
months,

" months, but my friends took care no-
" body should hurt me;—because,
" you must suppose, I was innocent.

" WHEN I came out of confinement,
" my friends were all in the country;
" so I was half naked. I went begging
" to the Tabernacle, and there I learned
" to say my prayers, and sing hymns;
" and the Saints took notice of me,
" and clothed me, and made me one
" of them.

" THEN I let my hair grow long,
" and parted it on the top, and tucked
" it behind my ears, and being sworn
" to secrecy, was introduced to their
" love-feasts:—and there they sat up
" all night;—and there at midnight all
" the lights were put out, to represent
" the darkness before things were cre-
ated;

"ated; and then every body pulls off
"their cloaths, to reprefent the ftate
"of innocence we are born in; and
"then we falute another promifcu-
"oufly, to prevent jealoufy; and to
"fhew that the Saints live in brotherly
"and fifterly love with one another,
"and as Adam and Eve had every
"thing in common among one ano-
"ther.

"Next I was fent down to a pri-
"vate houfe of worfhip in Norfolk;
"and there I preached fo concerning
"damnation, that I made all my
"hearers cry, groan, and grieve about
"it; and I talked about Hell, and the
"Devil, and roaring fires, fo dread-
"fully, that I ufed to put my congre-
"gation in fuch a heat, that I had
like

" like to have frightened them all
" into fevers.

" THEY ufed to give me money that
" I fhould not threaten them fo with
" damnation; fo I left off that fubject
" fome time:—but as I could not find
" any other out that anfwered fo well,
" I was going to my old ftory again,
" when a wicked woman took me be-
" fore the mayor, and fwore I wanted
" to ravifh her. Now fhe had given
" me encouragement, and feemed at
" firft as willing as I :—but rather than
" be expofed, I confented to go for a
" foldier.

" WHEN I was juft come into the
" army, I had like to have been hang-
" ed—becaufe, as we were marching
" in an enemy's country, I thought all
" I could

"I could lay my hands on was fair
"plunder :—only I had an officer who
"ſtood my friend. For you muſt
"know a very pretty wench, or maw-
"ther, as they call them in Norfolk,
"went abroad with me, who I had a
"child by while I was a Methodiſt
"Preacher; and as ſhe had ſome mo-
"ney, and her aunt had ſome good
"things which the niece could get at,
"and as it would have been a great
"ſhame for her to have been brought-
"to-bed at home of a baſtard child, I
"perſuaded her to pack up every
"thing ſhe could and follow me : and
"I ſtrengthened her conſcience with
"the interpretation of ſome texts that
"I choſe for my purpoſe; for I had
"learned how to do that at the Taber-
"nacle. For you muſt know every
"piece of ſcripture has two meanings:
"one

" one is the real meaning, which the
" Apostles designed it should signify;
" the other meaning is, that interpre-
" tation which every expounder pleases
" to put upon it, and which will best
" serve his own purpose; therefore
" there is nothing like the show of ho-
" liness for a person to get his own
" purposes served.

" Your people of true sense say,
" that pure religion is of the greatest
" simplicity, and that the poorest peo-
" ple may understand it, and that it re-
" quires no great explanation.—But
" that is not the religion I liked.—It
" is proper poor people should be con-
" fused, and kept in awe somehow;
" and therefore we took care, while I
" was a Preacher, to perplex and ham-
" per their minds pretty much; and

" to

"to hamper the poor is the proper bu-
"sinefs of us Reformers, as you will
"know by and by.

"Well, I told you I gave up my
"girl to the Captain.—I don't mean
"that I parted from her entirely; no,
"but the Captain used to come and see
"her very often: so then I used to go
"to the sutler's, or some such place,
"and stay there;—just as a great many
"people do now in London, who, when
"their wives have some particular vi-
"sitors, go out of town for a day or
"two, or sometimes let their wives
"go out of town for a day or two.
"Yet several of these husbands keep
"good shops in the City, and several
"live very genteely in and about St.
"James's, and are looked upon vastly
"well in their neighbourhood: and,
indeed,

" indeed, as England is a place of vaſt
" commerce, why ſhould not wives,
" daughters, ſiſters or nieces be tranſ-
" ferrable for ſome time, as well as
" other ſtocks are bought and ſold
" for time?

" My officer was killed, the war was
" ended, and over came I and my girl
" to England again. As we had ſaved
" ſomething, we took a public-houſe;
" and then I began to think about go-
" ing to the Tabernacle once more. I
" ſent my wife firſt, and a rare wench
" ſhe was at it. She did her part as well
" as if ſhe had been bred and born an
" actreſs; ſhe ſighed, and groaned, and
" cried, and turned up her eyes, and
" the Saints were ſo ſmitten with her,
" that they came to ſee me, and I
" kept a room for them on purpoſe,
" and

" and only she waited upon them; and
" happening to be chose Constable of
" the parish, by the Saints recom-
" mendation I was made Reforming
" Constable. But there was a fine-
" dressed gentleman used my house,
" who seemed sweet upon my wench:
" now, as he was not one of us, I was
" resolved he should pay four sauce.

" So the Saints and I consulted, and
" I lawfully married the girl; then
" caught him, as it was agreed on be-
" tween her and I; sued him for crimi-
" nal conversation; shut up my house
" to make my loss the greater, and re-
" covered swinging damages.

" I sell liquors now, but I don't
" take out a licence, 'cause only my
" Tabernacle friends visit me, and I
" don't

" don't want either to make their do-
" ings or my own public."

I DESIRED my new Keeper to tell
me, how he came firſt of all to fancy
he could make a Reformer?

HE replied, " Don't you know, my
" dear, that an old Smuggler makes
" the beſt Cuſtom-houſe officer? But
" my ſcheme, when I firſt returned
" from Germany, was, as I had ſeen a
" good deal of knocking-down work,
" and ſuch things, to have been a She-
" riff's officer, or a Thief-taker: but
" the Bum-bailiff's life I thought too
" ſcandalous; and as to the Thief-
" takers, I would have entered myſelf
" with them, only they would not allow
" me to go equal ſhares with them, un-
" til I had hanged three or four of my
" old

"old acquaintances, as they had done:
"fo I broke off my treaty, and ac-
"cepted of the place of Reforming
"Conftable; and it was the beft day's
"work I ever did in my life."

Upon enquiring how he could make it fo profitable, as he pretended to fay he did; he pulled out a pocket-book, which he called his *Weekly Journal,* and faid, "I'll fhew you, my dear, what
"my laft week's work was.

"*Sunday morning,* fix o'clock.

"Went to Morning-fervice at our
"Tabernacle. Spied a couple of Fleet-
"ftreet walkers dreffed clean, like fer-
"vant-maids, there. Took 1s. 6d. of
"them for hufh-money.
"Dis-

" DISCOVERED, as the firſt hymn was
" ſinging, a pick-pocket ſtealing a gen-
" tleman's watch. Seized the watch in
" the fellow's hand, but in the ſcuffle
" the thief got away. Purſued him,
" and never ſaw the owner of the watch
" afterwards;—becauſe I didn't come
" back that day to prayers, being ob-
" liged to ſerve God by looking after
" the fruit-ſtalls; and the gentleman
" imagining the thief had run away
" with the watch, I never advertiſ-
" ed it..

" ONE of the plyers belonging to the
" Society brought me word, that a new
" bawdy-houſe was opened the night
" before near the Strand, and that they
" had never ſent to us about it. Upon
" which we went down in a poſſe, and
" telling the maſter and miſtreſs we
" had

"had search-warrants, entered all the
"chambers. The beds were full with
"couples paired very lovingly:—the
"men (some of them) began to swear
"and threaten; but the girls and the
"mistress knew better how to deal with
"us; they made up a present among
"them, and then we went to dinner
"at my house to share the money.

"As it was some time before the
"meat would be ready, (which, by the
"by, we had seized that morning, be-
"cause the butcher's shop was open in
"sermon-time; it was a delicate fillet
"of veal, and a couple of fowls, which
"an old friend of mine a poulterer had
"sent in; bacon enough I was sure of,
"because one of my wife's best friends
"was a pork butcher; and as to greens,
"I had the choice of the market sent
"home

" home to me, 'caufe I, now-and-then,
" would not fee the green grocers fhops
" open, in our parifh, on a Sunday
" morning.—It is juſt ſo I obferve with
" their Worfhips; for tho' they take
" great pains to fupprefs bawdy-houfes,
" yet they do not like to be too crofs
" to their own neighbours)—Our din-
" ner, I fay, not being ready, and my
" wife faying fhe could like to eat fome
" fruit after dinner, we went out to feize
" the fruit-ſtalls; and in three quarters
" of an hour brought to my houfe two
" bafkets or fieves of currants, about ten
" fhillings worth of rafberries, and four
" maunds of other fruits worth about
" eighteen fhillings more. We took
" out enough for ourfelves after dinner,
" and put the reſt into the cellar; for
" we had people ready to buy all we
                              " took,

" took, as we allowed them good pen-
" ny-worths.

" In the afternoon, during divine
" fervice, becaufe the worfhip of our
" holy Religion fhould not be prophan-
" ed by fabbath-breakers, and to the
" glory of the Chriftian belief, and
" keeping the Commandments, as all
" vulgar folks efpecially ought to do,
" becaufe they will not like us be faved
" by grace—(for, Lord have mercy
" upon us! what are all the good things
" of this tranfitory life to the folid
" ones of for ever—"

I stared at him, as he was thus hypocritically holding forth. But this made me recollect the old proverb, that even the Devil can quote fcripture, if he wants his turn to be ferved by it.
I re-

I requested him to leave off Religion for the prefent, and go on with his hiftory, which he continued as follows :

" Having then not been long in the
" Reformation bufinefs, I was a little
" fhocked at our feizing one woman's
" fruit.—She lived in a cellar in Hol-
" born; and her hufband, a brick-
" layer's labourer, was ill at home in a
" fit of the rheumatifm. In the fame
" bed with him lay two of her children
" juft taken ill with the fmall-pox;
" herfelf was big with child, and ex-
" pecting to lay-in every day ; and fhe
" had, by parting with moft of her
" little furniture, made fhift to pur-
" chafe a very fine ftall of fruit ; and
" very neat it was fet forth on each fide
" the cellar-ftairs ; for fhe did not put
" it out into the ftreet. After we had
" feized

"seized it, the landlord turned
"her and her family out of doors that
"evening; and I said, as I was going
"home, I was almost sorry for the
"poor woman, she took on so much:
"but I was fined three shillings-
"worth of punch for that speech; for
"it was a forfeit, it seemed, though
"I did not know it before, for any
"one of our Society to shew signs of
"compassion.

"After church was over (for we
"always regulated ourselves by that,
"and by what their Honours said to
"us in the Vestry) we walked to New-
"ington, and there regaled ourselves
"with pies, tarts, tea, cheese-cakes,
"wine and punch, our bellies full,
"and put the bill up to the Parish-ex-
"pences; but we were forced to leave
"two

" two of our companions behind, they
" had drank fo much. As we came
" home over the fields, we were told
" there was a man dead-drunk on the
" grafs near us; fo we went up to feize
" him, and put him in the cage for
" getting drunk on the Lord's day. But
" feeing he was vaftly well dreffed, we
" confidered that he *mought* be fome-
" body of confequence; fo two of my
" companions took him in a coach to
" a Bagnio, got a bed there for him,
" and next morning went to fee how
" he did.

" THE Gentleman was very thankful
" for the kindnefs fhewn him, for he
" had loft his purfe with feven guineas
" in it; and he faid, if it had not been
" for their kindnefs, he fhould have
" loft

"lost his cloaths, and perhaps life; so
"he made them a handsome present.

"Now some prying lying fellows
"said, that my partners that *seed* him
"home had the purse; but I'll take my
"oath, if it was so, I had no hand in it.

"AFTER we returned to London, be-
"ing a little elevated with liquor,
"about midnight we took search-war-
"rants, and beat up about the Bawdy-
"houses in the Garden, and the streets
"adjoining."

HERE I could not help interrupting him by saying, I thought that by disturbing and frightening the people who used those places, they would not come again. But he shaking his head at me, told me, " Lord, child, one day or an-
"other

" other you'll know better; we only do
" it to keep the landlords in fear, and
" make them pay quarterage gene-
" rouſly.

" As to the whores, where would
" you have them go elſe? 'Tis their
" own market; and they muſt come
" there every night, though they were
" ſure to be ſeized every morning, or
" elſe ſit at home and ſtarve.

" BUT I'll tell you our method. When
" we come into one of theſe houſes
" where the girls are, we ſeize them
" all, and drag them out, to carry them
" to the watch-houſe. We won't let
" them have coaches, becauſe we pre-
" tend to ſay, walking will expoſe them
" more; but the true reaſon why we
" would have them walk is, THAT THEY

"May touch us as they go along, slily, and then as slily creep off. So all those that have money do; and out of twenty we take out of a house, we don't confine above four; and they are the pennyless strumpets, whose words we won't take, and who have nothing to put into our hands for security."

I asked him an account of these houses which he described to me. The account however which I shall give hereafter I hope will be more satisfactory to the reader, of *Tom and Moll King's*, the *Hazard Tables under the Piazzas*, the *Field of Blood*, *Weatherby's*, the *Golden Lion*, or *Cat*, *Bob Derry's*, and the *Night-houses* in and about the Theatres. But he so shocked me with his relations, and the actions

actions in which he had been concerned, that I could not bear to cohabit any longer with him; I was determined to starve first.

I HAD now some cloaths, not fine, indeed, but whole, plain and clean, and in which next morning I went to a Register-Office to enquire for a place.

WHEN I applied to the Register-Office for a service, I was recommended to no less a person for a mistress than JENNY DOUGLAS, who had, as I afterwards found, most of the clerks or masters of these offices in fee to recommend her *proper servants*.

I HAD heard much of her house, but was a stranger there; and as she had never seen me but in my brilliant days, and then only at a distance, she could not suspect, at least she did not suspect, that the person who appeared before her in a linen gown, plain holland apron, round-ear cap, black leather pumps, and coloured silk handkerchief, had ever been rolled along in her own chariot, in all the pomp and pride which the luxury of fashion could invent, and profusion could bestow.

I GUESSED for what intent I was hired, although I was retained as a chambermaid; but as I found my mistress had all the becoming hypocrisy necessary for a Procuress, I resolved to play her own game, and shew I could dissemble as well in my place.—She never suspected my having been upon the Town, and took more than ordinary pains to persuade me to give my company to some of her

best

best customers, promising me great things, and praising the life of a Kept Mistress, and how much it was preferable to that of a servant. But I knew too well that a Woman of the Town was the worst, the lowest, and the basest of slaves, condemned to do the most ignominious drudgery.——However, I suffered myself at last to be overcome, and consented to admit a gentleman to sup with me.

AND now, reader, behold me in that most miserable situation of a BAWDY-HOUSE PROSTITUTE; and if any part of a strumpet's life is more wretched, more pitiable than another, sure it is this. But that the reader may the better judge of our condition, it is proper to give him the following information.

When a long hackneyed ſtrumpet has been able to eſcape the common fatalities incident to her profeſſion;—ſuch as periſhing infected in hoſpitals, dying in the Marſhalſea, famiſhing upon a bulk in the out-ſkirts of the Town, or ſurviving tranſportation;—too haggard and unwieldy themſelves to gain any buſineſs by their own perſons, they immediately commence agents for others. From the experience of a ſeries of years, being acquainted with all the vices incident to both ſexes, and having minds prepared to perpetrate any enormity, they apply to ſome perſon who is called a Wine and Brandy Merchant, one perhaps of equal principle with themſelves; and who immediately puts them into a ready-furniſhed houſe in the environs of Covent-garden, and lays them in a ſtock of liquor. Being thus freighted, they

they are themselves to look out for the rest of their cargo; and enquire for three or four ladies to board and lodge with them.

Now there are three ways of gaining lodgers. The first is, that when some worthless fellow has, upon specious pretences, decoyed an inexperienced beauty from her friends, he hurries her to town, takes her to one of these brothels, revels with her there until he's sated, and then acquainting the mistress of the house with his intention, quits the helpless ruined victim for ever. This news is brought her by the Procuress: the deluded girl most commonly falls into fits, and for three or four days is in a strong delirium. When she recovers her senses, she is plied by the Bawd to *see* company, as it is called.

called.—She tempts her with promises; she terrifies her with threats; and I have known several reputable tradesmens' daughters perish for want in the Marshalsea, thrown in by sham actions by the Bawds at whose houses they have been left, because they would not consent to be public Prostitutes.

ONE day or other, perhaps, the hand of Authority may think it worth while to stop the rapid progress of such barefronted vice. I, altho' too long an actress in such ignominious scenes, detest the vile, the scandalous practices even to this hour, that are carried on in these Bawdy-houses, and which, to the disgrace of the Police, are encreasing annually within the precincts of Covent-garden.

ANOTHER

ANOTHER way which thefe miftreffes of houfes have of gaining lodgers is thus: On bulks and in allies we very often meet with girls about twelve or thirteen years of age, half naked, lying about in a moft defpicable condition. The inferior fet of Pimps, or more properly the Runners to the Pimps, when they obferve one of thefe poor objects with a pretty face, tempt them by a few halfpence, and the promife of a bellyfull of victuals, to follow them.

THESE fellows bring thefe poor creatures to one of thefe houfes: there the poor wretch is ftripped, wafhed, and clothed in fome ordinary things for the prefent; fhe is called a *Colt*; the Pimp has a pound or two for his trouble; and the girl, thus bought, is obliged to do juft as her purchafer pleafes.

THE third way is, when they have not immediately a supply from either of the above-mentioned methods, to engage three or four of the most *knowing* girls they can get to board with them, to keep custom to their house.

ALL these girls are used alike; they pay their governess half a guinea a week for their board; and out of every guinea which they get by a bedfellow, the Bawd has five shillings, which is called *Poundage*.

THEIR cloaths they hire of a tally-woman, with whom the mistress goes snacks in what these poor unhappy women pay; and I have known a girl pay eleven pounds for the use of a sack and petticoat, which when new cost but six guineas; and after that she was
thrown

thrown into prifon, and there died of the gaol diftemper, for the remainder of the tally-woman's bill, which was two pounds four fhillings more, for the ufe of the fame cloaths.

THE boarders in thefe houfes are obliged to fit up every morning (unlefs particularly employed) until four or five o'clock, for the good of the houfe, to drink with any ftraggling Bucks that may reel in at any of the early morning hours. With them they are obliged to fit—drink they muft—bear whatever behaviour thefe drunken vifitants are pleafed to ufe; and at laft, if they are in luck, put to bed to fome fellow who has fwallowed too many bumpers to fuffer him to be fenfible of the wretchednefs he muft inevitably endure from a moft impure connection.

In this situation I staid for some time; but as I had been already too much among mankind to entertain the most generous opinion of them, I only suffered myself to be won where I thought there was the greatest appearance of profit, and the least of danger. I had several *friends*, to each of whom I pretended *esteem*;—for *fondness* I found, with them, was too stale a bait to catch them.—They were persons who, as they told me, had seen the world, knew both man and woman kind, loved to please themselves, but were not to be taken in, they said, by a girl's flattery.

These were a set of persons of good fortune, who had, according to the phrase, run through the Town, and valued themselves upon their experience, their wit, their discernment, and fortitude-tude of mind. They liked me, becaufe, they told me, I had lefs cunning about me than any other of my profeffion, and was above being mercenary; but I ufed to laugh at them egregioufly when they left me. I found thefe men of wit and wifdom, as they called themfelves, to be my choiceft dupes: I always allowed them to be every thing they thought of themfelves, and then I made juft what I pleafed of them.

I PERSUADED them that, fo far from being mercenary, I was entirely difinterefted; and that was, by my often refufing a common prefent from thofe men, whofe vanity I knew would make them fhew the letters in which I fent their gifts back. Then I was always eager to lend thofe men ten or twenty guineas, whofe circumftances I knew were fecurity

rity good enough for a thousand times that sum, and whose weakness of understanding made them look upon such a proffer as the utmost effort of generosity; and such men were always uneasy until they had balanced with me, by behaving with a gratitude equal to what they called my liberality.

In two years which I lived at Mrs. Douglas's, by giving my company only to that set, or at least by persuading them that I was never happy out of their company, I had received from them above 500 l. For though there was not one of them who would not have challenged his best friend, if that friend should have surmised that a person who knew the Town could suffer a Woman of the Town to get a shilling from him; yet for such a girl as me, they told me, who

who defpifed money myfelf, and who loved men of wit and humour, as they were, they thought they could not do too much : but then, they faid, it was a free gift of their own, and not won from them by any fcheme, chicanery, or art of mine.—Poor men ! either wits or wife-ones, you are but purblind and fhallow-pated; and any woman who will fuffer herfelf to think, may make juft what fhe pleafes of the beft of you.

WERE I to recapitulate every acquaintance's behaviour, the relation would be odious, nay deteftable; but thus far I may be allowed to defend our fex, that we never fhould behave fo paffionlefs, fo inconftant, to thofe who pay us, did not their manner make us loath them. Only let us confider : Half a dozen men come into one of the Co-

vent-

vent-garden taverns, or bawdy-houfes; and after they think proper to fit down and be filent, a party of ladies are introduced, dreffed as well as their circumftances can afford, like Indian idols, glittering with green and red glafs about their necks and in their ears: indeed, Women of the Town are too much like thofe idols; they are dreffed forth only for a fet of favages. The converfation that enfues between thefe male and female groups is noify, obfcene, foolifh, or impertinent. It generally terminates in a quarrel among the men; or elfe fome of the women, who perhaps have not broke their faft that day, and yet will drink bumpers to fhew the ftrength of their heads and the foundnefs of their conftitutions, are foon intoxicated: they are fet together by the ears; this makes fine fun for the Bucks, who

who nobly and man-like ſtand by, and ſee three or four poor proſtitutes pull one another's cloaths to pieces, and with diabolical uproar exult on wretchedneſs being made more miſerable.

It is very common for every perſon to praiſe the times wherein they were young, and imagine that people were handſomer, wittier, and much more clever, while they had ſpirits and abilities to enjoy ſuch qualifications; but after they are grown old, they are apt to fancy the times are always degenerated. However, this I muſt ſay, that Covent-Garden, and its neighbourhood, is not the Covent-garden it was when I was young; and as a proof of it, I ſhall inſert a letter I met with by accident, which contains an abſtract.

Description of what Covent-Garden was, and what it is.

" To Mr. ————.

" I AM fick of London, and have been in it but a week. That Town which I ufed to hurry out of the country fo eagerly to come to, I am now preparing to leave; 'tis no more like what it was, than ideotifm is to be compared to wifdom.

" As to the people in general, their whole time is fpent in fruitlefs enquiries concerning things that can't concern them, or trifled away in endlefs diffipations.

" Covent-garden, once fo celebrated for its fun and fine women,
" is

" is grown as dull as any City Ward,
" and its Ladies of Pleasure are as vul-
" gar and as ugly as superannuated cin-
" der-sifters—all but LUCY—LUCY
" COOPER, indeed, still keeps it up in
" the old way. She is all and every
" thing as formerly; and altho' she
" needs no trumpet to sound forth her
" praises, she has one, she has.—But to
" pursue my former design, which was to
" let you know WHAT COVENT-GARDEN
" WAS, and WHAT IT IS, as far as I
" can in the compass of a letter, I will
" proceed.

" FORMERLY there were such Beau-
" ties upon the Town as the *Kitten*,
" *Bet Careless, Mrs. Stewart, Mrs.*
" *Howell, Peggy Yates, Sally King, Nanny*
" *Hall*, and several more very fine, or
" very pretty women. Then there was
" a house

"a houfe in Charles-ftreet, called *the*
"*Field of Blood*, where the droll fel-
"lows ufed nightly to refort; and then
"*Tom* or *Moll King*'s, a coffee-houfe fo
"called, and which ſtood in the mid-
"dle of Covent-garden market, was at
"midnight reforted to by all the Bucks,
"Bloods, Demireps and Choice Spirits
"in London.

"At *Tom King*'s you might fee every
"evening Women of the Town the
"moſt celebrated, and dreſſed as ele-
"gant as if to fit in the ſtage box at
"an Opera. There you were fure alfo
"of meeting every fpecies of human
"kind that intemperance, idlenefs, ne-
"ceffity, or curiofity could affemble
"together.

"In one of the rooms might be
"feen a group of grave-looking tie-wig
"wearers,

" wearers, half muzzy, eyeing afkance
" a poor fupperlefs ftrumpet, who lay
" faft afleep on the bench before them,
" her ragged handkerchief fallen from
" her neck, expofing her bofom bare,
" which thefe old letchers were gloat-
" ing upon.

" THEN you would fee *Tom King* en-
" tering, rough as a Bridewell-whipper,
" roaring down the Long Room, and
" roufing all the fleepers, thrufting
" them out of doors by the neck and
" fhoulders, if they did not immedi-
" ately call for fomething to drink.
" After he had fet his houfe to rights,
" three or four jolly fellows, claret-
" elevated, would enter and put it all
" into an uproar again. They would
" drink up one perfon's negus, overfet
" another's coffee, fnatch the leg of a
" goofe

" goose from a third, pull a fourth by
" the nose, kick a fifth's shins; till
" pell-mell, higgle-de-piggle-de all the
" guests in the Long Room were at
" battle-royal together.

" In one of the little rooms, (for
" there were two smaller or auxiliary
" drinking-rooms, besides what was
" called the Long Room) it was com-
" mon to have half a dozen ladies
" scratching one another for the posses-
" sion of a man, whose person they
" cared no more for than a sexton for
" a dead body, except for the perqui-
" sites. In the next room were as many
" men and women keeping it up jollily,
" making a Comus' Court there, and
" not heeding the next room's fray; for
" there, riots, bowls breaking, shriek-
" ing, murder, and such like amuse-
" ments

" ments were fo common, that I have
" known perfons fighting in one box,
" and at the fame time, in the box
" over-againſt them, another company
" drinking and being merry among
" themfelves, and not thinking it even
" worth their while to pay any attention
" to the belligerents, fo common there
" were fuch things as frays, fights, and
" fcuffles.

" ONE reafon that battles were fo
" much in tafte there, was owing to
" Boxing being then in its meridian at
" BROUGHTON's Amphitheatre; and
" our young fellows then, inftead of
" ftudying HOYLE to know how to
" play a hand of cards, were daily
" practifing with the Coachman, the
" Barber, and BROUGHTON, how to ma-
" nage their own hands.

" THERE

" THERE were then no disputes be-
" tween Majority and Minority, no betts
" on politics; no, it was only SMALL-
" WOOD againſt DIMMOCK, HUNT
" and JACK JAMES; TAYLOR againſt
" GEORGE, or GEORGE againſt JACK.

" AT this time the Town ſwarmed
" with three different ſorts of oddities;
" ſome of which were called CLEVER
" FELLOWS; ſome were called BOLD
" FELLOWS; and ſome, very ODD
" FELLOWS.

" THEN was the *Cyder-cellar* in
" *Maiden-lane* in great vogue; then
" HARRY HATSELL, SIM SLOPER,
" JOHN GEORGE COX, BOB WASH-
" BURN, HARRY SUMMERS, Doctor
" BARROWBY, JEMMY TASWEL, TOT-
" TY WRIGHT, and a regiment more
" of

" of frolic-making and frolic-loving
" beings; and, like Falstaff, were not
" only witty themselves, but the cause
" of keeping it alive in others. But the
" whole face of affairs in and about
" the *Garden* are totally changed. The
" fine women now are descended to
" street-walkers, and the only houses
" now encouraged are those kept by
" people of the most ignominious dis-
" positions: such as the CAT, where
" every enormity is nightly practised,
" that low-bred debauch and infamous
" ignominy can perform; where *Impo-*
" *sition*, with a most stupid visage, grins
" in your face; and where base fawn-
" ing *Vulgarity* waddles into the room,
" to swill the liquor about, and most
" filthily fulsome to flatter you out of
" t'other bottle.

"The women who live in lodgings and in jelly-shops now, about the precincts of the *Garden*, are a set of most ignorant, offensive, disease-beaten prostitutes, whose conversation is made up of the grossest obscenity, too rank to be heard by any but coal-porters.

"These strumpets are the refuge of suttling-tents and sea-ports, and what were formerly drummed out of camps and maritime towns, for infecting our sea and land subalterns; and who now palm their rottennesses upon the London Bucks for new faces. By the help of much white-lead daubings, carmine, tally-women's faith, and milliner's frippery, they appear
"like

" like fresh painted festoons upon mo-
" numents, tawdry coverings to cor-
" ruption.

" We no more meet casually with
" some hearty and really jolly droll
" fellows, with whom even prudence
" would now and then forgive our sit-
" ting up late; but the Town is now
" pestered with a crew of 'prentice-
" boys, Rakes, and Baby-bucks; such
" an unripened set of profligates as
" put even sinning out of countenance.
" Oaths sit aukward upon them, yet
" they are most terrible swearers. One
" night's drinking shatters their con-
" stitutions; yet they are always for
" gorging bumpers. They are for
" running any-body through the body
" over-night at the bawdy-houses; but
" the

"the next day in their shops, fall down on their knees trembling, if their master shakes his cane or rattan over them.

"I am, dear Friend,

"Your's sincerely, &c. &c."

END OF THE FIRST VOLUME.

www.ingramcontent.com/pod-product-compliance
Lightning Source LLC
Chambersburg PA
CBHW032056220426
43664CB00008B/1018